T5-AXT-244

The Pocket Guide to
WINDSURFING

Jeremy Evans

Bell & Hyman

The Pocket Guide to Windsurfing
was conceived, edited and designed
by Holland & Clark Limited

Designer
Julian Holland

Editor
Philip Clark

Artist
Nicolas Hall

Design Assistant
Martin Smillie

Photo Credits
Cover photograph by Alastair Black
Other colour photographs by Cliff Webb

Some of the artwork in this book
first appeared in *The Complete
Guide to Windsurfing* (Bell & Hyman)

Published by Bell & Hyman
Denmark House, 37/39 Queen Elizabeth Street,
London SE1 2QB

British Library Cataloguing in Publication Data
Evans, Jeremy
    The pocket guide to windsurfing
    1. Windsurfing
    1. Title
    796.1'24   GV811.63.W56

ISBN 0-7135-2355-7

Typeset in Great Britain by
Text Filmsetters Ltd, Orpington, Kent

Produced in Great Britain by
Purnell & Sons Ltd, Paulton

Contents

Part 1 Introduction

So you want to know all about windsurfing. It may seem a baffling sport, with a bewildering variety of boards and all kinds of other equipment, not to mention the specialized techniques required to handle a board in difficult conditions. However, the reality is fortunately simpler than that and (usually) great fun.

This book is designed as a basic windsurfing primer. It is aimed at beginners and near-beginners, as well as more experienced sailors who may want to brush up on things they have already learned. It includes enough information to enable you to get a wetsuit; a board and anything that's needed to rig it; and to learn to sail in a very short time (just a few days if the weather is right).

The more advanced section starts on page 52, and takes you through all the problems of sailing in stronger winds, with special emphasis placed on turning the board, and details of new techniques like the waterstart and the carve gybe.

One of the delights of windsurfing is that there is always something to learn and you can always get better. That means that you will constantly be running into problems – the board keeps heading up into the wind; it flips up on its edge; the rig pulls you over as you bear away – and in every case the answer is to refer back to the specific section in the book. Then you can go out on the water, try again, and get it right.

Happy windsurfing!

Glossary of Windsurfing Terms

ABS/ASA Popular plastic skin materials for board mass production. Trade names for this material include Copex (Fanatic) and Polycoren (Mistral). It is quite different from the other major skin materials, which are polyethylene and *glassfibre*.

Allround This generally refers to a *flatboard* that can be used for learning, fun, racing, and strongish winds. The Windsurfer Regatta is an excellent example.

Apparent wind The wind experienced by the board moving across the water. It is a combination of the *true wind* and the wind created by the board's movement.

Battens Flat pieces of flexible *glassfibre* used to support the *roach* of the sail.

Bearing away Turning the board away from the wind.

Beating Sailing as close to the wind as possible.

Beaufort Scale A scale of wind strengths from Force 1-12 used by weather forecasters (*see* page 26).

Blank A foam blank is roughly the shape and size of a board. It is shaped into a *custom board*.

Blow moulding The polyethylene skin of the board is blown into a mould on the same principle as blowing up a balloon.

Boardsailing Another name for windsurfing, used primarily because the Windsurfer is a brand name.

Break A surfing term for where the wave starts breaking. 'Shorebreak' is when it breaks on the shore.

Buoyancy aid Not to be confused with a lifejacket, which is designed to prevent you from drowning when unconscious.

(Most lifejackets are too bulky for windsurfing.)

Camber The amount of fullness in the sail.

Carve Carving a turn is achieved by banking the board like a ski. The technique is solely for use in strong winds with the *pintail* style of board.

Cavitation See *Ventilation*.

CE The Centre of Effort – where the power of the wind is centred in the sail.

Chord An imaginary straight line describing the shortest distance from the *clew* to the mast.

Cleat A fitting used to secure a line. The 'Clamcleat' is generally used for windsurfing.

Clew The corner of the sail which is attached to the end of the wishbone.

Clew-first Sailing with the rig reversed so the clew points into the wind. Used in *freestyle* and sometimes to help *gybing*.

CLR Centre of Lateral Resistance – the main point about which a board will turn, which in most cases means the *daggerboard*.

Custom board A one-off, handmade from a foam *blank* laminated with glassfibre.

Daggerboard Used to stop the board going sideways. There are three main types:
1. *Dagger* As used on the original Windsurfer Regatta. Is either left down, or has to be pulled up by hand.
1. *Pivoting* Swings back beneath the hull, but does not retract.
3. *Retracting* Retracts fully or partly into the hull.

The elements of a windsurfer are common to most models, particularly if they are of the allround type illustrated here. You may find slight general differences, and more marked differences in specific parts such as the mast foot and daggerboard – but otherwise all boards are much the same.

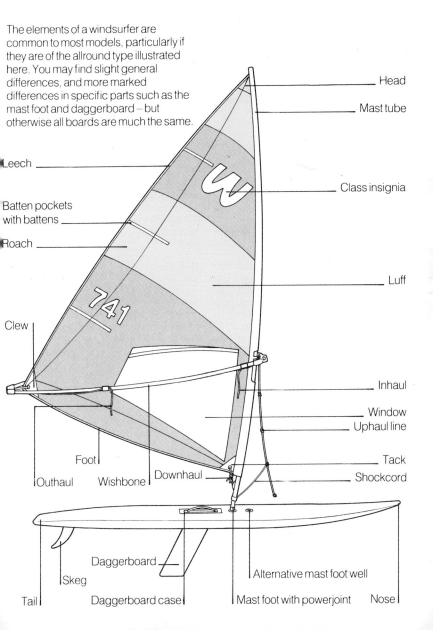

Head

Mast tube

Leech

Batten pockets with battens

Roach

Class insignia

Luff

Clew

Inhaul

Window

Uphaul line

Tack

Shockcord

Foot

Outhaul   Wishbone   Downhaul

Daggerboard

Skeg

Alternative mast foot well

Tail   Daggerboard case   Mast foot with powerjoint   Nose

Depression Period of unsettled weather which frequently means strong wind. Also called a 'low'.

Displacement A loose term which usually refers to a Division II Open Class board which has a rounded hull – only part of the bottom is immersed and it therefore displaces less water.

Downhaul line Attaches the *tack* of the sail to the mast foot.

Drysuit A windsurfing suit which is completely waterproof.

Epoxy A high strength resin, which is usually used in conjunction with polystyrene foam.

Fathead Sails with very wide heads that need to be supported by one or two battens are called fatheads, fullheads, powerheads, etc. They are for use with funboards in moderate to strong winds.

Fence A foil on a *skeg* designed to prevent *ventilation*.

Fin Another word for skeg.

Flatboard A board that is flat, and by definition an *allrounder* which is easy to sail.

Floater A funboard term for a board that has enough *volume* to support your weight when stationary.

Foot The bottom of the sail.

Footstraps Straps to put your feet into so that you stay connected to the board. Only used for stronger winds.

Freestyle Tricks on a board, usually performed within a three-minute routine which is marked on style and technical ability.

Funboard The general name for a board specifically intended for strong winds.

Gasket A strip of rubber or plastic which prevents water surging up through the *daggerboard* case.

Gate start Sometimes used when starting a large fleet in a race. All the boards cross the line behind a 'pathfinder' sailing on the port tack.

Glassfibre Woven glass which is laminated with a resin (either epoxy or polyester) to form the hard skin of a board.

Gybing Altering course so the stern of the board passes through the eye of the wind.

HAR High Aspect Ratio: a sail which is short in the *foot* and long in the *luff.*

Harness A device that enables you to hook on to lines attached on either side of the *wishbone*, and lean back with the rig taking your weight.

Head up To sail up towards the wind – usually by inclining the rig towards the tail.

High A high-pressure weather system which usually means settled weather and light winds.

Hypothermia Acute loss of body heat which can lead to death. Hypothermia can occur very quickly in UK waters and is extremely dangerous.

IBSA International Boardsailing Association, which administers international Open Class racing.

Inhaul The line used to lash the *wishbone* to the *mast.*

Ins-and-Outs A competition that involves

reaching back and forth round a series of buoys.

IWS International Windsurfer Schools – the originators of the most popular teaching system.

IYRU International Yacht Racing Union, which administers all types of yacht racing.

Knots Nautical miles per hour. A nautical mile is 2025 yards or 1.15 statute miles (1.85 km).

Leash It is vital that the rig is connected to the board by a leash in case the mast foot pulls out.

Leech The outer edge of the sail.

Le Mans start A racing start with all the boards lined up on the water's edge.

Leeward The side of the board the wind is blowing away from. Opposite to *windward*.

Leeway The amount the board moves sideways.

Lip The crest of a wave where it's just breaking.

Long distance race A marathon race of at least ten miles.

Long john The most popular style of windsurfing wetsuit.

Low A depression – unsettled weather and wind.

Luff The edge of the sail from the *head* to the *tack*. Next to the mast tube.

Luffing Heading up into the wind.

Marginal sail A smaller sail for use when

it's blowing too hard for a full size regatta sail. It frequently has no *roach* and needs no *battens*.

Mast Either glassfibre or alloy. Most masts are about 14¾ft (4.50 m) long.

Mast foot The mast foot is connected to the mast by an articulated powerjoint which is usually a simple rubber coupling (*see Universal joint*). Every manufacturer seems to have a different size or shape.

Mylar Sailcloth with a plastic film for lightness – for enthusiasts only.

Neoprene The rubber used to make wetsuits.

Non-slip Most boards have a nonslip finish moulded into the deck. Its effectiveness varies considerably.

Nose The front end of the board.

Offshore wind Wind blowing away from the shore.

Olympic Triangle The normal racing course for boards.

One-design A class where all the boards are the same.

Onshore wind Wind blowing on to the shore.

Open Class Different boards conforming to the same measurement rules; divided into Division I (*flatboards*) and Division II (*roundboards*).

Outhaul Line to pull the *clew* of the sail out to the end of the *wishbone*.

Pintail A strong wind design with a pointed tail designed to make the board *carve* turns.

Plane To skim over the water.

Polyester The conventional resin used in a glassfibre laminate.

Polyethylene A hard-wearing plastic skin material.

Polystyrene/Polyurethane Two types of foam used for the solid filling of boards. The former is lighter but more brittle, and is usually laminated with epoxy resin; the latter is stronger and heavier and in much wider use.

Port Left – indicated by the colour red. 'Port tack' is when the board is sailing with its port side to *windward*.

Powerjoint *see* Universal joint.

Pumping Moving the rig back and forth to create wind.

Rail The side or edge of the board.

Railing When the board flips up on its side.

Reaching Sailing with the wind blowing across the board.

Roach The sail area which is outside a line drawn between the *clew* and *head* of the sail. It has to be supported by *battens*.

Rocker Curvature of the bottom of the board running from nose to tail.

Roto-moulding Moulding *polyethylene* by rocking and rotating the mould containing the plastic.

Roundboard A racing board with a round underwater profile.

Running Sailing with the wind almost directly behind.

Scoop Another name for *rocker* at the nose of the board.

Shims Friction pads which hold the *daggerboard* rigid in its case.

Shockcord Elasticated cord which prevents the sailor from losing the *uphaul*.

Sinker A board which doesn't have enough volume to support the weight of a sailor unless it's planing.

Skeg A small fin at the tail of the board which keeps it sailing straight.

Spin-out The result of *ventilation*.

Starboard Right – indicated by the colour green. 'Starboard tack' is when the starboard side of the board is to *windward*.

Storm daggerboard A shorter daggerboard which makes the board more easy to handle in strong winds.

Tack The corner of the sail by the *mast foot*.

Tacking Turning the nose of the board through the eye of the wind. A board sails on a 'tack' – either *port* or *starboard*.

Tail The back of the board.

Tandem A board for two people.

Terylene Used to make most sails.

Tides Coastal movements of the sea induced by the pull of the sun and moon. Tides should be treated with great respect by windsurfers.

Trim Trim of the board is the relationship between *CE* and *CLR*; 'trimming the sail' is letting it in and out to match the direction of the wind.

True wind The wind blowing over the land or water, as opposed to the *apparent wind*.

Universal joint The UJ is the connection between rig and board which allows the rig to be swung through 360° and inclined through 180°. It can also be called the *powerjoint*.

Uphaul The rope used to pull the rig up out of the water.

Ventilation At high speed, air travels along the bottom of the board and then down the *skeg* causing it to lose its grip on the water. The result is a *spin-out* as the tail of the board slides away from the wind.

Volume Boards range in volume from under 100 litres to over 300 litres. The heavier the sailor, the more volume his board needs – the specialized sinker is the exception.

Waterstart The method of starting a *sinker*, which can also be used with a conventional board.

Weight groups At a regatta, contestants are frequently divided into weight groups to make for fairer competition.

Wetted area The area of the bottom of the board which is in contact with the water. The less wetted area, the less drag, and the faster the board will go.

Windsurfer The original Windsurfer is a trade name, which is why some people talk about 'sailboards'.

Windward The side of the board the wind is blowing on to – the opposite to leeward.

Wishbone Composed of two 'booms', made from elliptical alloy tubes with plastic/nylon end fittings.

Types of Board

Apart from 'custom' boards which are individually made by hand, all boards are mass produced in factories, with Germany and France being the major suppliers in the world market.

The conventional construction technique used on 99% of boards is for a solid foam core to be covered in a hard plastic outer skin. This can be polyethylene (the toughest), ASA/ABS (superior cosmetically), or glassfibre (the cheapest to manufacture).

Whether or not a board is the most up-to-the-minute design is largely irrelevant to all but the most enthusiastic and advanced sailors. The major manufacturers offer a well-presented product which is a simple variation on that offered by their competitors. Every now and again one manufacturer gains a temporary advantage, but construction and marketing techniques are so sophisticated that there is really very little to choose between the different products.

Boards and rigs go hand in hand. If your sailing is likely to be limited to the occasional weekend and the odd holiday, a good allround flatboard with a standard rig will probably be quite sufficient – though you would be advised to invest in a second sail, using the bigger one when the winds are light, and a smaller one when they get stronger.

At the other end of the spectrum there is the fanatical enthusiast, who may be either rich or supported by a manufacturer. He (or she) will change his boards and equipment with every fluctuation in fashion. With a bewildering variety to choose from, he can suit his sailing to all kinds of weather conditions and every eventuality. At the very least his inventory will run something like this:

He likes racing, therefore he has a high volume Division II Open Class racing board with a special rig and two racing sails.

When there is no Division II racing he likes to race his one-design – Windsurfer Regatta, Mistral Competition, etc – and, besides, it's a good board for freestyle.

The wind goes over Force 4, so it's out with his short funboard. If he's good he has an ultra low volume sinker which gives more precise handling characteristics in strong winds.

With his funboard he has a special rig with three or four sails ranging from 38 to 60 sq ft (3.5 to 5.6 sq m) – and a variety of wishbones (or an adjustable version) to suit every size. He also likes funboard racing or just cruising and going fast in a straight line, so he has a funboard which is longer and has a daggerboard – it's frequently called a Pan Am board because of the annual Pan Am Cup in Hawaii.

For those who fall somewhere between the occasional sailor and the fanatic, the sensible middle course is to have one board for light or moderate winds; and a funboard that's designed specifically for use when the wind exceeds Force 4. Between the two are the allround-funboards which are claimed to do everything – but they're seldom any more than acceptable compromises which will not do everything perfectly.

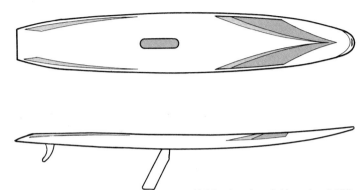

Allround Board

The type of board that started it all, and is still the best to learn on and is the most popular for general use. Flat, stable, and forgiving, almost every manufacturer has a board like this in his range.

Normal dimensions are around 12½ ft

(3.80 m long); weighing about 40 lb (18 kg); with a sail between 65 sq ft (6 sq m) – full size or regatta – and 50 sq ft (4.7 sq m) – allweather. The skin materials can be polyethylene, ABS/ASA, or glassfibre, while the core is almost always polyurethane foam.

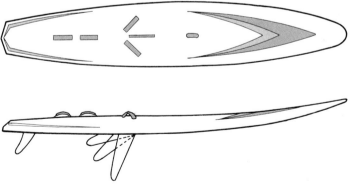

Allround-Funboard

A more modern compromise between the allrounder and the funboard, it retains the stable, flat bottomed shape with high volume for good stability and flotation. However, it changes the trim by a variety of means: a larger skeg; a smaller

daggerboard sited further back; the mast foot sited further forward, and possibly adjustable with a mast track.

These changes prevent the board luffing and make it more manoeuvrable in strong winds, at the expense of performance in light winds.

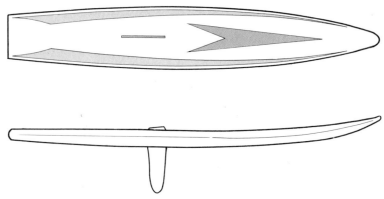

Division II Open Class

The Open Class roundboard is the fastest type of board that is raced round an Olympic Triangle. Its rounded shape allows it to plane quickly, but makes it unstable and difficult to sail in waves or stronger winds. The boards have very high volume (over 300 litres) to make them plane easily, but this makes them difficult to manufacture down to the weight limit of 40 lbs (18 kg) and so consequently they are expensive.

Division I of the Open Class is for flatboards, which are easier to sail.

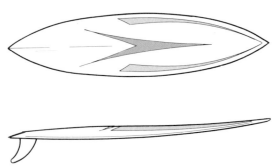

Funboard/Sinker

The characteristics of a funboard are:
Short length, 10 ft 10 ins (3.30 m) down to 8 ft 2½ ins (2.50 m).
Light weight, as little as 15½ lbs (7 kg) for a custom board.
Low volume and a pintail profile.

No daggerboard, but either a single skeg or three skegs and footstraps.

The most extreme version is the sinker, which cannot be tacked (too short and too little volume) and must always be carve gybed. The rig cannot be pulled up – the sailor always has to waterstart.

A 'sinker' jumps into the sunset. The venue is Pozo, on the island of Gran Canaria.

A wave board gets airborne in the surf off Sylt in West Germany. The sailor is American Ken Winner.

Boards gybe round a buoy in a World Cup regatta at La Torche in north-western France. Racing is held in minimum of Force 4.

Types of Rig

The rig drives the board, and if you are to enjoy your sailing it is vital that you have the correct gear. Always choose a sail which is the right size for your capabilities – avoid being over-powered.

1. A small hollow leech sail of around 4.0 sq m (43 sq ft) suitable for Force 5+.

2. An 'allweather/marginal' of around 5.7 sq m (60 sq ft) for general use up to Force 5.

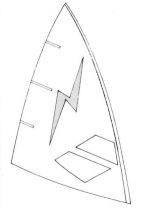

3. An Open Class 'regatta sail' with an area of around 6.3 sq m (68 sq ft).

4. The new style of 'fullhead' funboard sail has a short wishbone and high clew.

Above: The three main components of the mast foot are bolted together. They are: the foot itself (**1**), which plugs and locks into the well; the rubber powerjoint (**2**); and the top fitting (**3**).

Clothing

Wetsuits

The most basic windsurfing garment is the wetsuit, which may be 3, 4 or 5 mm (about ⅛th to ¼ in) thick, depending on weather conditions. A tight fit is important, for your warmth relies on there only being the thinnest layer of water between your body and the neoprene. However, you must also be able to stretch and expand your muscles.

Right: The long john is the most popular style of wetsuit for summer windsurfing in northern waters. When it gets colder you can put a nylon windbreaker or a neoprene bolero on top, which will help cut down wind-chill. Alternatives for summer use are a 'short john' with short legs, or a one-piece suit with short arms. Zips make the suit easy to put on but bump up the price, and are prone to corrosion.

The alternatives for winter windsurfing in northern waters are a better wetsuit or a drysuit. The drysuit keeps all the water out by means of waterproof material used in conjunction with watertight seals at the neck, wrists, and ankles. Winter wetsuits are blind stitched, which means that both panels and stitching are watertight. The resulting garment is not waterproof, but is less clumsy than a drysuit.

Left: The conventional drysuit is a baggy garment which is rather ungainly on the open sea. A newer style is made of tight-fitting black neoprene which looks and feels better.

Shoes

It is more fun sailing barefoot, but you often need a shoe or boot. For a beginner, these protect against bashes, and the non-slip sole makes up for poor board surfaces (different boots suit different decks – it's difficult getting the right one).

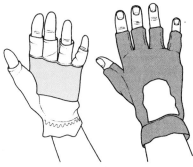

Gloves

Unless you have a problem with the skin of your hands, gloves should never be necessary in summer. However, in winter they can take the bitter chill off your fingers. The choice lies between leather-palmed neoprene gloves which soon get soaked; neoprene mittens which are warmer; and a fully waterproof glove (trickier to get on).

Harnesses

The harness takes the weight off your arms, but encourages you to be lazy. Top racers avoid using them, but for the leisure sailor they are great energy savers.

   The harness should support the back, with a quick release system for the buckle so that you can get it off and over your head in a hurry – for instance if you're trapped beneath the sail with the harness line caught round the hook.

   Some harnesses have positive buoyancy which is generally accepted by yacht clubs who insist that buoyancy must be worn. A back-pack on your harness enables you to carry spare lines and extra clothing.

Carrying the Board

Don't try carrying a board on an ordinary car luggage rack. You must have a proper windsurfer rack which will carry up to four boards side by side and on top of one another.

Make sure the rack is properly padded (try an ironmonger for rubber insulation tubing) and do not pull the board down too hard with the straps – it is surprisingly easy to cause serious structural damage. For the same reason you should pad the wishbone where it touches the board.

Always load in the same way. Make sure the roof rack is firmly attached. Lift up the board (easier with two people than one) and place it, deck down and nose forward, on the rack, taking care it is not blown off by the wind. Place the wishbone on top of the board; and the mast on top of the wishbone with the mast foot removed. Finally, secure the board with the ties.

Invest in a set of board straps for tying down the board (above). Take the free end of the strap over the board and wishbone, under the rack on the far side, back over the board where it can take a turn round the mast, and down round the rack on your side, where you can finally pull it tight (below) and secure. The buckles must not be allowed to rub against the skin of the board: if they do, you must pad them.

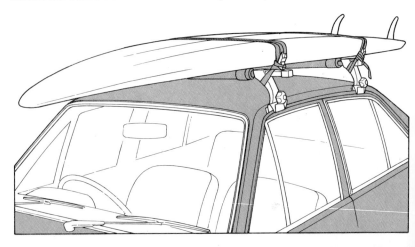

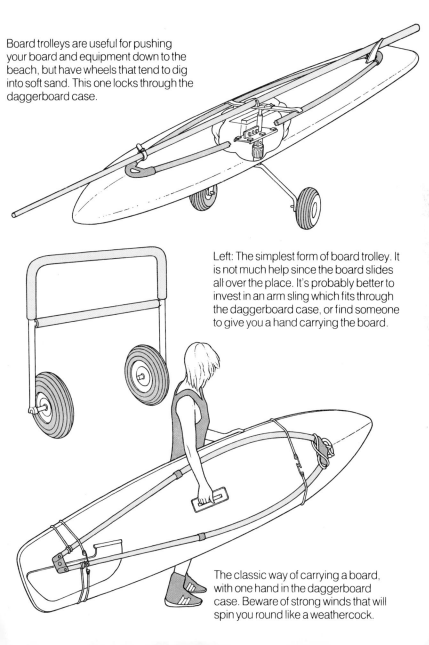

Board trolleys are useful for pushing your board and equipment down to the beach, but have wheels that tend to dig into soft sand. This one locks through the daggerboard case.

Left: The simplest form of board trolley. It is not much help since the board slides all over the place. It's probably better to invest in an arm sling which fits through the daggerboard case, or find someone to give you a hand carrying the board.

The classic way of carrying a board, with one hand in the daggerboard case. Beware of strong winds that will spin you round like a weathercock.

Basic Theory

The Centre of Effort (CE) is the area where the wind's force is concentrated in the sail. The Centre of Lateral Resistance (CLR) is the point about which a board is designed to turn. If the CE and the CLR are in equilibrium, the board will travel in a straight line – the shape of the board, the daggerboard, the skeg, and the rig have all been designed to this end.

However the designers of boards cannot allow for wind or wave conditions. A sudden gust of wind has the effect of shifting the CE further back in the sail, which causes the board to head up towards the wind unless you take action to prevent it from doing so – you must rake the rig forwards and sheet in.

Waves are more difficult to deal with. They throw the board off course in an unpredictable manner – ideally you should learn to handle a board on flat water before you need to worry about mastering waves.

Steering

You steer the board by raking the rig forward or back. Rake it forward and the CE will push the nose of the board away from the wind, so that the board bears away, turning about the CLR. Rake it back, and the CE will push the tail of the board away from the wind causing it to turn in the opposite direction – it *heads up*.

Running requires a slightly different technique. The wind is directly behind you, and the rig is held at 90° to the board. You still incline the rig to steer the board, but you do it to one side or the other, rather than foward or back.

Inclining the rig to leeward makes the board head up towards the wind: inclining it to windward makes the board bear away from the wind, until you are forced to gybe on to the opposite tack.

Sail Drive

When the wind blows on to a correctly trimmed sail, the air flow separates and passes on either side. On the leeward side (the one furthest from the wind) the air flow is accelerated by the curve which has been built into the sail. The result is a reduction in air pressure.

Meanwhile, the high pressure area on the windward side of the sail (closest to you and the wind) pushes towards the low pressure and generates drive.

The drive is roughly at right angles to the chord of the sail – an imaginary line drawn between the mast and the clew of the sail. Its efficiency in propelling the board will depend on your skill, and your course in relation to the wind – close hauled, reaching, or running. For reasons that will be explained on the following pages, close hauled and running are slower than reaching.

Apart from sail drive and the skill of the sailor, a board's performance is also affected by several other factors – principally its shape and construction; its trim as determined by the relationship between the skeg, daggerboard, and mast foot; and its size and shape.

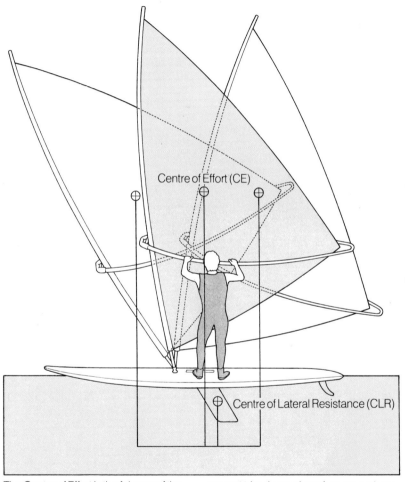

Centre of Effort (CE)

Centre of Lateral Resistance (CLR)

The Centre of Effort is the fulcrum of the wind's force in the sail. It is largely determined by the design of the sail (a sail with a short foot has the CE further forward), how stiff the mast is, and the prevailing weather conditions. If the CE is directly over the CLR, the board is 'in trim' and will travel in a straight line. However, correct trim depends on factors such as the design of the board; the relative position of the mastfoot, daggerboard and skeg (which is the reason for fully retracting daggerboards and mast tracks); and the variety of weather conditions. Different trim is needed for different winds.

Sailing Conditions

When choosing where and when to go sailing, safety and common sense should be prime considerations. If it's your first attempt, there are a number of factors which could be enough to put you off for good. Don't go out if it's freezing cold; blowing too hard; flat calm with no wind; or if there are waves breaking on to the beach. However, the greatest danger for a windsurfer is being blown away from the beach. An offshore wind will get progressively stronger as you get blown out, and as you find you can't cope, you'll spend more and more time in the water, getting pushed in a direction you don't want to go at an ever-increasing speed. The end result is that you will (hopefully) be rescued.

An offshore wind is unsatisfactory for the beginner (near the shore will be very gusty, due to

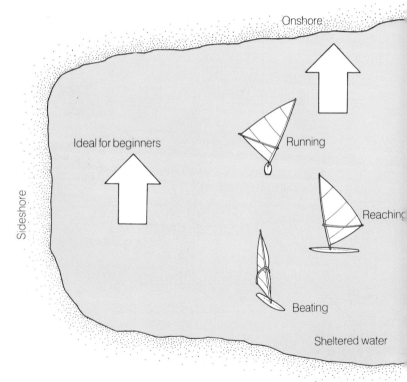

Onshore

Ideal for beginners

Running

Reaching

Sideshore

Beating

Sheltered water

the wind being filtered by trees, houses, etc), but an onshore wind can be as bad. The wind heaps up waves, and depending on how the bottom shelves, these can easily build up into surf with a fierce undertow – conditions which are dangerous, and frequently result in broken masts, wishbones and daggerboards. Whenever possible, go for the ideal compromise which is a sideshore wind.

In the drawing of a lake below, the sailors have a choice of onshore, offshore and sideshore winds. Those launching sideshore can 'reach' across the lake; those launching onshore will go on a 'beat'; and those launching offshore have a 'run' in gusty winds.

Conditions will be similar on the sea, but you must also take tides into account. They can be very dangerous, so check them out first.

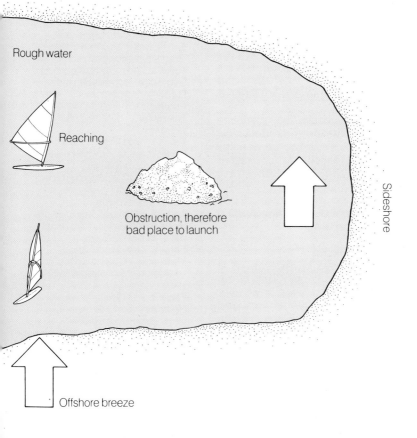

Rough water

Reaching

Obstruction, therefore
bad place to launch

Sideshore

Offshore breeze

Weather and Forecasting

As a windsurfer, you are interested in wind – as you become better you will learn to curse the weather when there isn't enough of it.

Wind and weather are also vital safety considerations, and it's therefore important to keep in touch with weather forecasts and have enough basic knowledge to interpret them.

The forecasts are available every day, but unfortunately none of them are specifically designed for windsurfers. You will learn most from the weather maps published in the newspapers, and from tuning in on the radio to hear the shipping and inshore weather forecasts, which supply details on wind strengths and the likely weather pattern.

You can also use the telephone to listen to the pre-recorded local coastal area forecasts, or perhaps best of all phone up a Weather Centre – the larger ones are manned 24 hours a day – where the forecaster will be quite happy to chat about your windsurfing weather prospects.

Weather Patterns

Wind is created by differences in atmospheric pressure. This is responsible for the overall weather pattern, but a more localized phenomenon occurs when the sun heats up the land more quickly than the sea – it creates a *low* which sucks the air from the *high* over the sea, which creates an onshore breeze building up along the coasts in summertime, starting up around midday.

The Beaufort Scale

The wind is measured on the Beaufort Scale, invented by Admiral Beaufort in 1805. The units are knots, which are nautical miles (about 1.85 kilometres) per hour. The descriptions are for life on the open sea, and it won't be so extreme inshore which is where windsurfers tend to sail.

Force 0 1 knot or less. Calm, mirror-like sea.
Force 1 1-3 knots. Light air. Gentle scaly ripples.
Force 2 4-6 knots. Light breeze. Small wavelets. May have glassy crests but these will not break.
Force 3 7-10 knots. Gentle breeze. Large wavelets. Crests begin to break. Posibly some white horses.
Force 4 11-16 knots. Moderate breeze. Waves becoming longer with white horses.
Force 5 17-21 knots. Fresh breeze. Moderate waves with white horses and possibly occasional spray.
Force 6 22-27 knots. Strong breeze. Large waves forming with extensive white crests and spray.
Force 7 28-33 knots. Near gale. Sea heaps up and foam from breaking waves is blown in streaks.
Force 8 34-40 knots. Gale. Moderately high waves. Edge of crests break into spindrift. Well-marked streaks.
Force 9 41-47 knots. Severe gale. High waves. Confused breaking crests. Spray affects visibility.
Force 10 48-55 knots. Violent storm. Exceptionally high waves hiding ships from view. Sea covered in white foam.
Force 12 64 knots plus. Hurricane. Air full of driving spray. Very bad visibility.

Rules of the Road

Before you hit the water, learn the *Rules of the Road* designed to prevent collisions when afloat. Use them when you're on your board, but also use common sense – it is frequently stupid and unfair to try to force a large yacht to give way, and 'power gives way to sail' must be tempered by the fact that it may be difficult for a powerboat to alter course, while you can turn in an instant.

The following are the main rules, which can be taken as gospel when you meet another board:
1. *Starboard tack has right of way over port tack.*
2. *The overtaking craft keeps clear.*
3. *When two craft converge on the same tack, the one to leeward has right of way.*

1. Larger craft have right of way over smaller ones! Never get in the way of commercial craft, and treat any motorboats or yachts with respect if they're negotiating a channel – you don't have right of way, and you could end up with a summons.

2. If the dinghy bears away, the board will have right of way since it is to leeward of the dinghy and sailing a higher course. However, if the dinghy is racing and the board is not, it would be courtesy for the board to give way.

3. Starboard (the dinghy) has right of way over port (the board), though once again courtesy about craft racing or common sense may apply. Remember that others may not know the 'Rules of the Road' or how to behave.

Knots

A windsurfer is rigged with rope (or lines), using knots and cleats to make the ends secure.

Apart from the thick uphaul rope, all the line can be the same. The manufacturer of the board will usually provide a full set, but if you need to buy your own make sure it is a high quality pre-stretched Terylene designed specifically for yachting purposes. It is quite expensive, but if you buy cheap rope it may wear badly; slip when it shouldn't; or burn your hands in an unpleasant way.

Also be sure that you buy the correct diameter – about ³⁄₁₆ in (5 mm) – to fit through the holes and jam correctly in the cleats.

All rigs have variations with cleats, pulleys and jammers – you may not need to use all these knots, but they are useful to know.

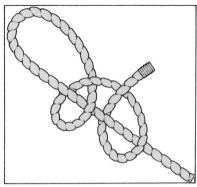

Above: A round turn and two half hitches can be a useful way to tie off the inhaul line if you don't have a cleat, but are more often used to secure the downhaul line to the tack of the sail – this depends on whether the downhaul is a simple length of line, or comes ready equipped with cleats and pulleys to pull it down.

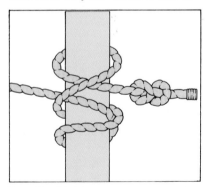

The rolling hitch is a very secure way of attaching the inhaul line to the mast. It pulls tighter and tighter so that it won't slip – the only disadvantage is that it pulls so tight that you may need a marlinspike to undo it, when you wish to change sails and alter the height.

The bowline can be used to make a loop in the downhaul line so that you can get a double or treble purchase when you pull it tight. As with two half hitches, you may not need to use a bowline if special cleats and pulleys are provided on the mast foot assembly.

Right: The figure-of-eight is tied in the end of a line so that it can't slip out through a cleat if it becomes unjammed – very important for the outhaul.

Below: The simplest inhaul lashing is a loop passed round the mast – pull it tight until the overhand knot (or alternatively a figure-of-eight) is hard against the mast. The disadvantage is that it may slip down the mast.

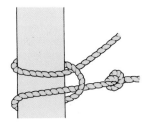

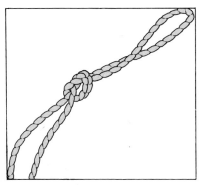

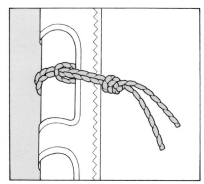

The Double-ended Knot
Many French boards are equipped with a wishbone that has a U-shaped notch cut in the wishbone end-fitting. You slip on the inhaul lashing as above, but then tie a single overhand knot in both free ends. With the wishbone lying parallel to

the mast, you can slip this knot into the notch. When you pull the wishbone up to the correct horizontal position (using the outhaul) the inhaul lashing is pulled tight to the mast. This is quite adequate for general leisure sailing, but too sloppy if you take it seriously.

Assembling the Rig

The basic rigging sequence is:
1. Slide the mast into its tube.
2. Put the mast foot in the base.
3. Attach the downhaul line.
4. Attach the inhaul line.
5. Put in the battens (if any).
6. Attach the wishbone.
7. Attach and pull out the outhaul.
8. Attach the uphaul and shockcord.
9. Tighten the downhaul and trim the outhaul until the sail takes up its correct shape.

The rigging sequence can be varied according to the rig, but to save wear on the sail you must always apply luff tension after tensioning the outhaul.

Right: Before sliding the mast up the tube, check if there is an extra fitting at the tip of the mast – Mistral have one which is designed to spread the head of the sail. Push the mast right up to the top – if by any chance the luff tube is too long, you will need a taller mast or a mast extension which can be adjusted to the right height, so that the cut-out is at eye level.

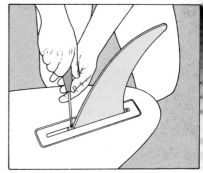

Above: Putting in the skeg (most screw in). The best system is the universal fin box which accepts all shapes and sizes with the same box fitting.

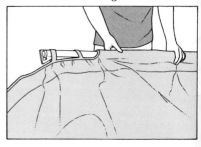

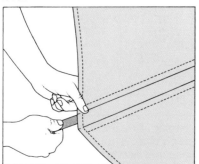

Slide in the battens. There is usually a fold in the cloth on the leech which secures them in the pocket.

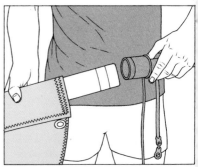

When you put in the mast foot, take great care to remove sand and grit which may jam it solid.

Attaching the Downhaul

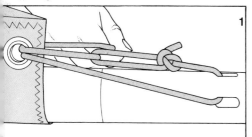

1. You can use a bowline to make a loop in the downhaul line, so you get some purchase between the loop and the hole in the tack (cringle).

2 and **3.** When it's pulled tight, the end can be tied using two half hitches.

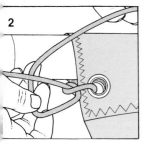
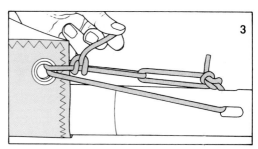

Attaching the Uphaul

The thick uphaul line is usually pushed through the large hole in the wishbone end fitting and secured by an overhand knot. If it is conventional rope, make overhand knots for handholds.

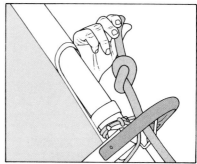

Attaching the Inhaul

Sailors are becoming more and more aware of the importance of lashing the wishbone rock hard to the mast – it makes control of the rig much easier.

Unfortunately it's very difficult unless you have a well-designed wishbone end-fitting with 'cheeks' that lock either side of the mast – if you don't, you will have to work out your own failsafe method.

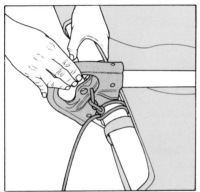

1. With the inhaul line tied to the mast, rest the wishbone in the correct position – it should be approximately eye height when sailing.

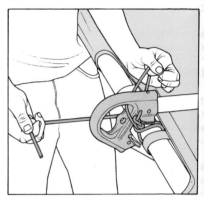

2. Take the line through one side of the handle (through the hole if there is one), and back and round the mast on the underside.

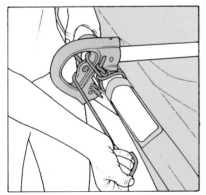

3. The line now passes through the other side of the handle – at this point pull it tight by rotating the mast back and forth with your free hand.

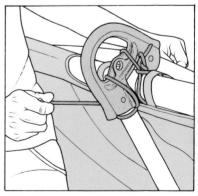

4. The line can now be secured to a cleat, or secured round the wishbone with a couple of round turns. It should be rock hard if you use this system.

ttaching the Outhaul

you buy a new board, you may
ave to tighten the cleats. They
ave self-tapping screws, and can
nly be secured if they are
edded on the rubber-covered
on-slip part of the wishbone.

The outhaul system shown in
ese pictures is used on 90% of
oards, but it is really unnecessari-
complicated. If the sail has a
ew handle which you can pull on,
single cleat right down by the
nd fitting will suffice, and if there
no cleat you can make the line
st with two half hitches, though
ey will pull very tight.

The only advantage of having
e cleats halfway along the wish-
one is that you can adjust outhaul
nsion while sailing, though this is
eldom necessary.

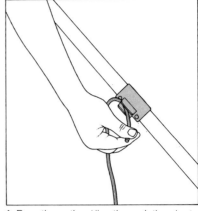

1. Pass the outhaul line through the cleat on one side of the wishbone and jam it securely with a figure-of-eight knot tied in the end. Lead the free part back to the end fitting, through the roller, and up to the clew.

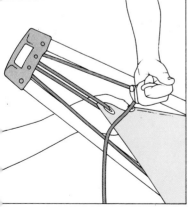

. Pass it back again to the end fitting, rough the other roller, and up to the leat on the other side. You can then pull tight as required (remember to secure e end).

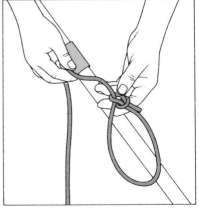

3. If you want to adjust the outhaul line under way (possibly for racing) make a large loop by putting a bowline in the line – it makes it easier to grab and pull on.

Carrying the Rig

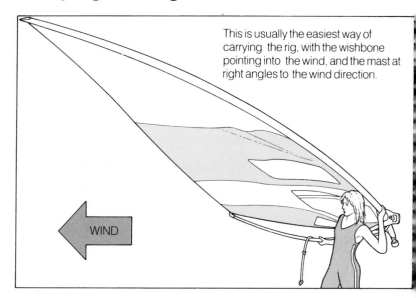

This is usually the easiest way of carrying the rig, with the wishbone pointing into the wind, and the mast at right angles to the wind direction.

WIND

Before taking to the water, jam the mast foot into the ground (sand is ideal, or you can stick it in the board with the skeg removed) pull the rig up, sheet it in, and see what it looks like.

If there are horizontal creases try more downhaul/less outhaul; if there are vertical creases try more outhaul/less downhaul.

Carry the board into the water, and lock the mast foot securely so that it won't come out unless there is danger of breaking the mast or your foot. Make sure the rig is leashed to the board, and there is no chance of losing it.

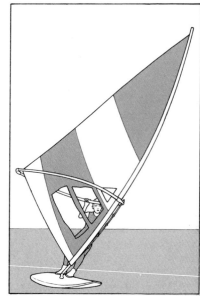

Right: By removing the skeg you can rig the board and practise on dry land. Place the board at 90° to the wind, sheet in and lean back.

Uphauling (Rig to Leeward)

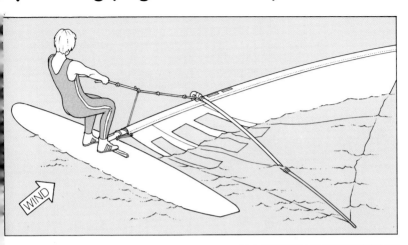

1. With the wind behind you, place your feet together on the centreline of the board (usually either side of the mast foot).

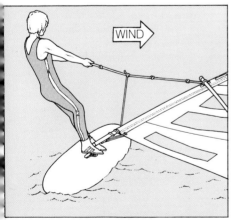

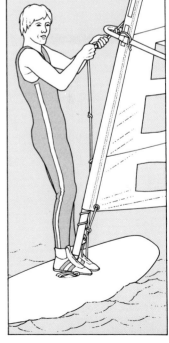

2. Keep a straight back with your knees slightly bent, and pull until the rig starts to lift out of the water. If the wind is not directly behind you, it will make the board and rig slew round until it is.
3. Continue to pull until the clew is free of the water.

Uphauling (Rig to Windward)

When you uphaul the rig, it is relatively simple if it is downwind (to leeward) with the wind behind you. However it may be upwind (to windward) – usually because you have fallen off – when the board always drifts downwind of the rig. You have to learn to uphaul it partially on the windward side, and then get it round to the leeward side where it can be uphauled in the conventional matter.

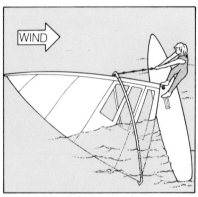

1. With the wind blowing towards you, lift the rig until the tip comes clear of the water – this will be quite difficult.

2. With the wind coming from slightly ahead, it begins to lift the sail, and swings it over towards the tail of the board as the tension gets lighter.

3. With the clew pulled clear of the water, the sail swings across the tail (or the nose if the wind was blowing from the tail).

4. The sailor steps round from the leeward to the windward side of the board, letting the rig blow round into the right position.

Turning the Board

When it's blowing hard you need to be very quick and deft when uphauling with the rig to windward. As an alternative, you can let the clew drag in the water, while the wind in the sail turns both board and rig until the sail is in the correct position. You will soon discover how the board reacts to the rig. Lean it forward and the board will bear away. Lean it back and the board will head up.

1. With the clew free of the water the sail behaves like a flag so the rig is always blowing downwind on the leeward side of the board.

2. By inclining the rig forward the sailor can make the board bear away. If he inclined it back, the board would *head up* (*see* page 45).

3. The sailor has to take small steps round the mast foot, as the rig swings round the nose of the board, always blowing downwind.

4. He can turn the board through a full 360° in its own length, just by inclining the rig into the wind without hindering the board as it turns.

Getting Under Way

A lot of people have problems with the weight of the rig when they're pulling up the sail. It always seems heavy until all the water has drained out of the mast tube; and

until the clew lifts clear of the water, which has the effect of de-powering the sail. Pull it up quickly – and then get your balance and rest.

1. Get your balance, with your back straight and knees slightly bent. Next, let go of the uphaul and hold the mast with your front hand.

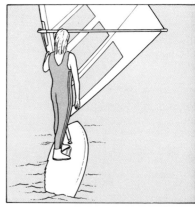

2. Incline the rig well to windward. Face forward with your front foot just behind the mastfoot, and your other foot further back.

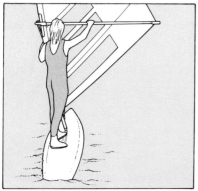

3. Reach out and grasp the wishbone with your back (sheet) hand. Continue to balance the board with the rig inclined to windward.

4. Move your front (mast) hand to the mast, and pull in evenly on the sail which will get you under way. Lean back as necessary with straight arms.

Stopping

When you get under way, you sheet the sail in until it stops flapping. Keep the rig raked well forward, and if the board shows any inclination to head up (luff) rake the rig further forward and sheet in. If you don't, the board will carry on heading up until the wind hits the leeward side of the sail, pushing you over and into the water.

If the pull of the rig threatens to drag you over, lean back to counterbalance it, with arms straight and evenly spaced. When the time comes to stop, let the rig pull you upright and gradually let out your sheet hand until the sail starts flapping and loses power – then transfer your hands to the mast. You can then lower the rig and rest before trying again.

1. Once you sheet in, the board will start moving. A beginner's greatest problem is that the board invariably heads up into the wind – to counteract this tendency, incline the rig forward and sheet in the sail.

2. When you want to stop, you can do so in a hurry by letting go with your sheet hand. You can then let the sail flap, and lower the sail by holding the mast or uphaul.

3. As soon as the rig touches the water, the board will come to a dead halt. You are now in a perfect position for uphauling again. Stopping is better than colliding with other boats.

Sailing in a Straight Line

When sailing in a straight line, you will become aware that the direction of the wind appears to change. This phenomenon is most apparent at high speeds, and is caused by the difference between *true wind* (the wind experienced by someone standing still) and *apparent wind* (the wind experienced by the sailor).

If a windsurfer is sailing towards a true wind of 15 knots at a board speed of five knots, he will be sailing towards a wind which is his own speed added to the true wind – an apparent wind speed of 20 knots.

If he is sailing away from a true wind speed of 15 knots at a board speed of five knots, the apparent wind hitting his sail will be the true wind less his own speed – 10 knots of apparent wind.

Whenever you're sailing on a windsurfer, you will experience winds which are more or less than the true wind speed. With the wind behind you it is less, and consequently you go rather slowly; when sailing directly towards it, the wind speed may double.

As your speed increases, the more the apparent wind will change in direction. Thus, a board reaching at 20 knots will have its sail trimmed far tighter than one travelling at 10 knots, even though they are both sailing in exactly the same true wind. You can see this when overtaking a yacht.

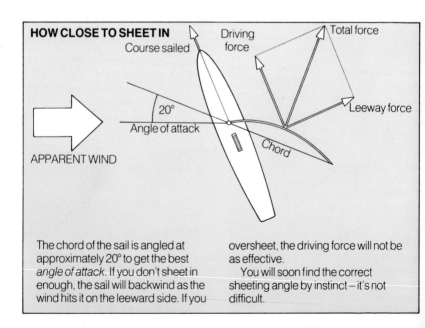

HOW CLOSE TO SHEET IN

Course sailed

Driving force

Total force

20°

Angle of attack

APPARENT WIND

Leeway force

Chord

The chord of the sail is angled at approximately 20° to get the best *angle of attack*. If you don't sheet in enough, the sail will backwind as the wind hits it on the leeward side. If you oversheet, the driving force will not be as effective.

You will soon find the correct sheeting angle by instinct – it's not difficult.

The sail's drive is determined by its *camber*, which is the degree of fullness in the sail represented by the area between chord and sail in the illustration opposite. (The amount of camber is decided by the cut of the sail, the bend in the mast, and the tightness of the outhaul and downhaul.)

To find the correct *angle of attack* (or *sheeting angle* – the word 'sheet' refers to the mainsheet of a sailboat) the sail should be trimmed so that its chord is no closer than 15-20° to the apparent wind. If it is closer, the air flow will break away into turbulence to leeward, which will brake rather than suck the sail; if it is not sheeted in enough, the air flow will shift to the leeward side and the sail will backwind and lose efficiency. Eventually you will be able to trim

Above: Perfect trim on an allrounder. Note that the hands are evenly spaced, pulling on the rig with the Centre of Effort between them, so that they share the strain equally.

You can use overhand or underhand grips. Most sailors use an overhand grip for the back hand, changing to an underhand grip for the front hand – due to the shape of the boom, it spreads the grip more evenly over four fingers.

the sail by instinct. You can then learn to tune the amount of camber in the sail – broadly speaking you need a full sail for light winds, a medium-full sail for moderate winds, and the sail pulled as flat as possible for stronger winds. (Obviously, all this depends both on the size of the sail and on your individual style of windsurfing.)

The Three Points of Sailing

Close Hauled/Beating
Sailing towards the wind, you would expect to be pushed sideways and backwards. The aerodynamic shape of the daggerboard combats this tendency, converting the movement into forward drive.

There are exceptions to this general rule. In strong winds, experts can sail funboards upwind with a single skeg, but they rely on speed and even then won't point very high towards the wind.

Reaching
When the wind is on the beam (ie at or near 90° to the board's course) there is less sideways drive and less pressure on the daggerboard. Consequently, this is always the fastest point of sailing.

Running
One would expect sailing with the wind behind to give the most drive. Not so, the apparent wind is lessened and with the wind only hitting the sail on one side there is no low pressure area. Consequently the sail is pushed rather than sucked, while the air flow around the edges suffers from turbulence.

Running is usually the most difficult point of sailing.

When running, you stand square on to the board with the rig at right angles to it so you can look ahead through the window. You steer by inclining the rig to windward (to bear away) and to leeward (to head up), but keeping your balance can be extremely difficult, especially if there are any waves.

Beginners find sailing close hauled (beating) the most difficult point of sailing. The answer is not to attempt to sail too close to the wind. This often results in the board heading up, losing power in the sail and dropping you into the water. Always remember to keep the rig well forward!

Reaching with the wind 'on the beam' can be anything from a *close reach* to a *broad reach*. It is the easiest point of sailing for beginner or expert – you simply concentrate on sailing a straight course with your weight a little further back, trimming the sail according to wind direction.

Sailing a Course

It is very necessary practice for a learner to be able to sail in any direction – not just on a reach, which is always easiest, but downwind or upwind to get home.

You should practise sailing in a complete circle. (**1**) Bear away from a reach to a run. (**2**) Gybe on to the opposite run. (**3**) Head up on to a reach. (**4**) Head up some more on to a close reach and then a beat. (**5**) Tack on to the other beat when you find you can't sail directly into the wind, but have to pursue a zig-zag course of alternate tacks. (**6**) Bear away on to a reach. (**7**) Continue on round the circle.

If you are unable to sail on every point of sailing, you are unable to go out without rescue at hand. The learner usually finds beating most difficult, which is why offshore winds are dangerous.

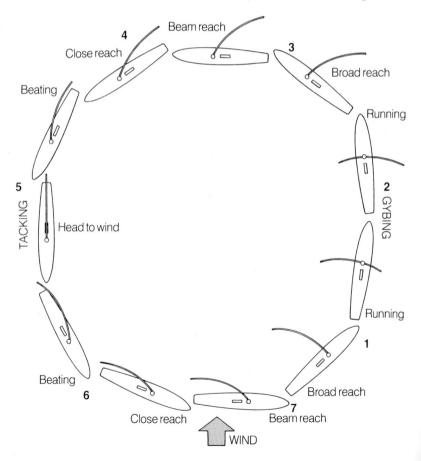

Heading Up

You can alter course on a board as easily and rapidly as with the rudder on a boat. Weather conditions make a difference. If it's blowing hard with big waves and you're sailing a sensitive board, it will react instantaneously, while other boards are considerably more sluggish.

To head up, you rake the rig aft and sheet in until you are on a beat. In light winds you will then have the wishbone close to your body with your arms bent, while in stronger winds you can lean back with your arms fully stretched.

Knowing how much to head up is difficult for the learner. You can head up as close as possible to the wind, but not so close that it begins to strike the sail on the leeward side. If you do, the board will then round up so that it is facing directly into the wind. The result is that you must either step round the mast or fall in.

Below: When you head up on to a beat, you can normally sail within 30° of the apparent wind – it depends on your skill, as well as the board and rig you are using. Sail as high as possible, until the sail is beginning to flutter just a very little between the window and the mast.

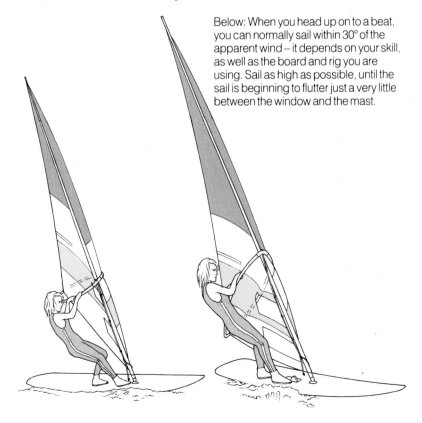

Bearing Away

To bear away, you need to rake the rig forward, gradually letting out the sail as the wind goes further behind: eventually you end up sailing downwind on a run with the wind directly behind and the rig at right angles to the board.

While bearing away, it can be difficult to keep your balance. Bearing away from a beat to a reach, the board will accelerate, and the power in the rig may threaten to pull you off your feet –

plant them firmly, lean back against the pull, and crouch down in order to keep your balance.

Be prepared to move your weight inboard as the sideways pull on the sail lessens – at this point it's normal to find there's nothing supporting you and you fall in to windward. Giving some sharp pulls with the sheet hand helps you to accelerate the turn and keep your balance. Don't pull too hard, however.

You can make a conventional board bear away if you push down on the windward side (rail). Conversely if you push down the leeward rail it will head up. This is a technique which is much used in Division II of the Open Class – the round hulls are highly responsive to this kind of steering, but it requires an experienced sailor to stay in control.

Footsteering is a different technique (*see* pages 68-69).

Below: To bear away from a beat to a run, the sailor rakes the rig forward and into the wind (**1**). This will make the board bear away on to a broad reach. As the board alters course the sailor moves his weight inboard and lets out the rig to keep it at the correct angle to the wind (**2**). When the wind starts coming from behind he has to be very careful not to fall in to windward (**3**) and must take up a position behind the sail from which he can see through the window. Finally, when sailing on a run downwind (**4**) he keeps the rig square to the wind and inclined to windward so that he sails a straight course. He moves his weight back on the board where he can get better balance and better leverage on the wishbone.

Basic Tacking

In order to sail towards the direction the wind is coming from, you need to follow a zig-zag course. This is called tacking. You sail on one tack and then the other (port and starboard) as it suits you. Governing factors may include: prevailing conditions, obstructions *en route*, and tacking for the sake of a change. Start on either tack.

When you decide to change tacks, rake the rig aft to get the board turning up into the wind. Continue to do so until the end of the wishbone starts to pass over the centreline of the board. Then drop your mast hand from the wishbone to the mast, start to move round the front of the mast foot, and drop your other hand.

Standing on the centreline of the board, continue holding the mast with the one hand and swing the rig over the tail of the board until it's on the right side for the new tack. Swinging the rig clew first towards the wind helps perpetuate the turn in the same way as the turning sequence on page 37. At this point you can rest and get your balance.

Change hands on the mast. Continue to move round to the other side of the board until you are in the right position for getting under way, and rake the rig well forward so that the board will bear away on to the new course, ready for you to sheet in and sail off on the new tack. Raking the rig forward will keep the board turning.

Finally, get under way again. Reach out for the wishbone with your sheet hand while moving your feet behind the mast foot; incline the rig to windward and face forward; place your mast hand on the wishbone; pull in with equal pressure on both arms and the board will sail off in a straight line.

With skill you can change from one tack to another in well under 10 seconds. Keeping your balance is hardest when you move round the front of the mast without the stabilizing influence of the rig to pull on.

If you have problems getting under way on the new tack, remember to incline the rig forward before sheeting in.

Gybing

When you gybe, you change tacks by
turning the tail of the board through the
eye of the wind. In its simplest form,
gybing is one of the easier manoeuvres.
1. Sail on a dead run, inclining the rig to
windward so that the board bears away.
2. As the tail passes through the eye of
the wind, let go with the sheet hand.
(Alternatively, if the wind is light, push
with the sheet hand to make the board
turn.)

3. The rig flips over across the nose of the board.

4. Having turned the rig through 180° (you may need to swing the rig to make it turn) grab the mast with the old sheet hand which becomes the new mast hand.

5. Rake the rig to windward, and grab the wishbone with the new sheet hand.

6. Put the new mast hand on the wishbone, and sheet in, sailing off on the opposite reach.

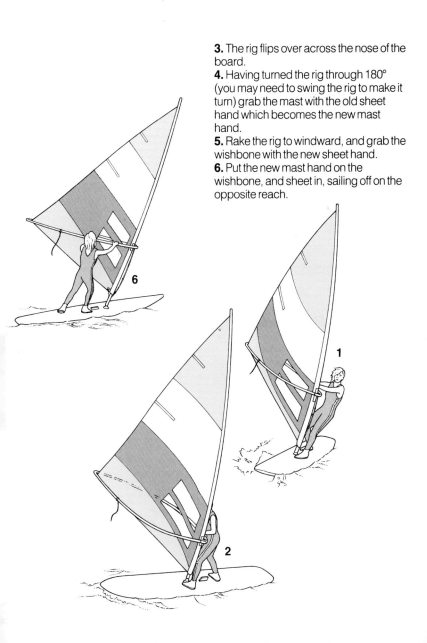

Part 2 SAILING IN STRONGER WINDS

Once you feel confident sailing in light winds, you are ready to move on to greater things.

Racing
You may like to try the thrill of racing in the keenly-contested Open Class, or in one of the manufacturers' one-designs. Either will give you the chance to qualify for international regattas.

Funboard Sailing
You may like to sail a funboard in strong winds, learning to use footstraps and developing your sailing skills so that you can footsteer, carve high speed turns, jump from wave to wave, master the duck gybe, and learn to sail a sinker.

Freestyle
A very different speciality is freestyle (performing tricks on a board). There's not always enough wind to sail a funboard, and flipping the board up on to a railride or pirouetting while you duck tack are pleasant diversions in fine weather.

Beyond these specialities, there's always something to learn. Safety is a very important factor. You've got to take care of your sails and equipment; learn how to launch in surf; and maybe even become an instructor.

That's the great thing about windsurfing. You can set your aspirations as high (or as low) as you want.

Some More Theory

A sailing boat heels over as the force of wind increases, effectively cutting down its sail area and potential forward drive – it also begins to make greater leeway (travelling sideways) due to less projected keel area.

In the same wind a windsurfer reacts differently. The board remains flat on the water so that maximum daggerboard area can still be projected, and by means of the articulated powerjoint the rig is heeled *into the wind*.

This process cuts down the projected sail area while the drive remains the same; the sailor has much more leverage (the greater the wind the more the rig is heeled over) and the rig also creates lift, which has the effect of

making the board lighter on the water, and more ready to plane.

When you first try, it takes a lot of faith to cant the rig to windward and hang beneath it. However if you can't hold it standing upright, there is no option – lean back, pull it over on top of you, and you'll soon get used to a great sensation.

Strong Wind Difficulties

Force 4 is very different from Force 2, and beyond that Force 6 is very different from Force 4!

Everything happens so much quicker. With the wind holding the rig down and several gallons of water trapped in the sail and mast tube, pulling it up seems like an immense weight. Your strength is sapped, and if you don't move fast

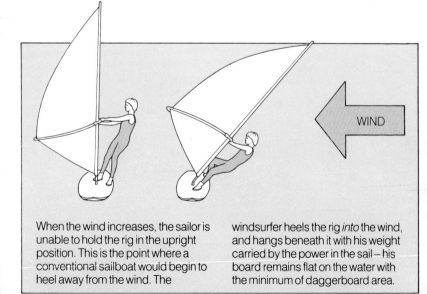

When the wind increases, the sailor is unable to hold the rig in the upright position. This is the point where a conventional sailboat would begin to heel away from the wind. The windsurfer heels the rig *into* the wind, and hangs beneath it with his weight carried by the power in the sail – his board remains flat on the water with the minimum of daggerboard area.

when you get it up, the rig is blown from your hands by a gust and you have to start all over again.

There are also waves, making the board extremely unstable, and combined with cold water and a chilling wind, windsurfing can become a bleak prospect.

The Answers

Strong winds are handled by technique and equipment. Physical fitness is important, but unless you want to be a top competition sailor there is no need to be stronger than the average person who can run for a bus – 100 yards that is, not 10!

Mastering the techniques is largely a matter of understanding the theory, but beyond that it is a fantastic help to have a good board and equipment. You must learn to handle a harness; use high wind sails (with a high clew and short wishbone with less leverage); and use a board that has footstraps and is trimmed for high winds with a smaller daggerboard and large skeg(s) set well back so that there is no chance of inadvertent luffing.

Finally, to get the most out of strong winds, buy the best gear.

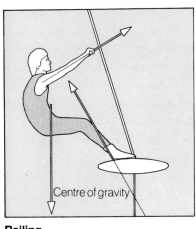

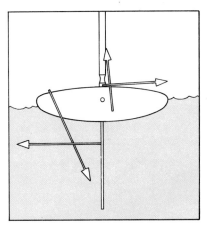

Railing

The sailor hangs on to the wishbone, with his centre of gravity (represented by the vertical arrow) well outboard.

The combined effect of the long daggerboard passing through the water and the push of the mastfoot leads to a phenomenon called *railing* – if unchecked the board will flip up on its side (the rail) and completely capsize.

The sailor therefore has to push down with his feet to counteract this tendency.

If railing persists, he will have to move his feet further outboard to get more leverage. After that the only answer (apart from sheeting out and losing power) is to reduce the daggerboard area, which is usually achieved by retracting it.

Trim and Daggerboards

In stronger winds the trim of the board is very important. A standard allrounder performs well up to around Force 4, but beyond that it may suffer from lack of stability, and becomes very prone to heading up into the wind whenever there is a gust.

The more modern allround-funboard solves these problems in a variety of ways. The adjustable sliding mast foot is a recent development which makes the *trim* of the board infinitely adjustable. However, the most worthwhile developments have probably come in fully-retractable daggerboards.

Left: For boards without a fully retracting system, the simplest answer is an alternative 'storm daggerboard'. It is fixed in position but is much shorter than the conventional dagger, and will alleviate any problems of aquaplaning or lack of control on the run.

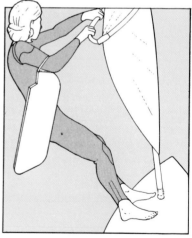

Until recently the Windsurfer Regatta was one of the few boards which was only available with a daggerboard that lifted straight up and down.

This kind of non-retracting daggerboard leads to several problems in stronger winds. On a fast reach the dagger will *aquaplane* causing the board to rail up on its side (capsize) and lose control; and on a run the length of the dagger will tend to take control of the board's course, causing severe problems if there are waves.

To counteract this difficulty Windsurfer sailors have to 'pull' their daggers and carry them.

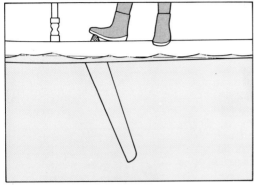

A modern fully-retracting daggerboard with a slim foil. Operated by a simple foot action, it is designed to be fully down when sailing upwind. With the narrow foil and relatively small area of the dagger, you should be able to control any tendency to rail by pushing with your feet on the side of the board – if you can't, retract the dagger back a little.

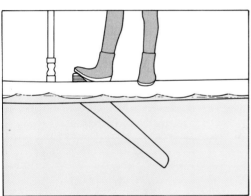

The dagger is half retracted for sailing on a close reach. The board would be more easily controlled with the dagger fully retracted, but on this point of sailing the board will make a lot of leeway which you can't afford to lose if you are racing or in a hurry to get home.

If sailing gets too difficult, retract the dagger even further.

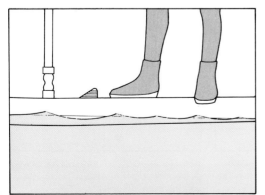

Here, the dagger is fully retracted, with the daggerboard case sealed by a rubber slot gasket. This should prevent any water from shooting up through the case.

Sail on the runs with the dagger in this position, and if you have a funboard, retract the dagger fully on any point of sailing broader than a close reach.

Harness Techniques

The harness is a marvellous invention. You hook in and hang from the wishbone, and with all the strain taken off your arms you can sail for miles.

Before you try a harness you should be a proficient sailor in Force 4. You have to be able to sail if your harness line breaks (it happens now and then).

Inexperienced sailors can get into some very dangerous and unpleasant catapult falls while hooked into the harness; and you still need to develop your arm muscles – it's impossible to use a harness on a run, and undesirable on a reach when you're racing.

Finally, a word of advice. Most top sailors seldom hook in. The longer you postpone the harness, the better your technique will be – and when you try it, see how it feels on dry land *first*.

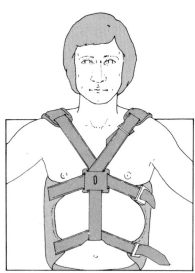

Above: The harness should support your back. It must have a quick-release buckle so that you can get it off in a hurry if you get tangled in the line.

To hook in, come to a close reach, dip your knees, and at the same time pull the wishbone sharply towards you to flip the

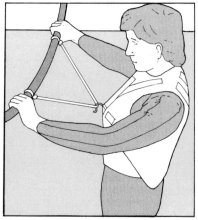

harness line into the hook. (Some hooks point upwards.) Lean back and take your weight on the harness.

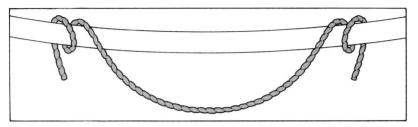

Above: There are various ways of attaching the harness lines to either side of the wishbone. Your hands should fall near the ends of each line.

Right: The simple knot illustrated here works well and is unlikely to come undone so long as it is pulled tight.

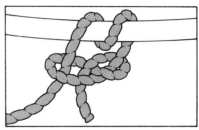

Harness Lines

The harness lines should be pre-stretched Terylene of around $\frac{3}{16}$ in (5m) diameter. They should be around $3\frac{1}{2}$ ft (about 1.10m) long, depending on whether you like them long or short.

The position of the lines will need to be adjusted according to the wind conditions. If it is windy they need to be further back, as the CE moves back into the sail. As the wind diminishes you should move them forward.

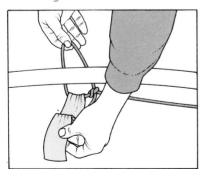

The easiest way to attach harness lines is with specially made Velcro tabs. The loop passed over the wishbone; the Velcro tab goes through it and locks

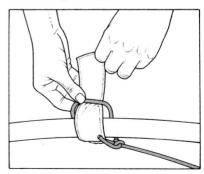

back on itself; then the line is pulled tight. The tabs are easy to adjust, relatively cheap, and widely available from windsurf shops, with replaceable lines.

Launching in Stronger Winds

Launching in stronger winds can be difficult. If the wind is offshore the water will be flat, but the wind may be gusty. If the wind is onshore there will almost certainly be breaking waves which may amount to 'dumpers' that break on top of you with a fierce undertow following.

For a safe and successful launch, you must choose your place and the prevailing conditions. A deeply shelving beach is the cause of dumpers, so you should find a gently shelving shoreline – in tidal areas that frequently means launching only at low water.

When you have chosen your spot, watch and get a feel for the rhythm of the waves so that you can choose the best time to launch. If possible, the wind should be blowing across the shore (side-shore) with a maximum tolerance of 45° either way.

Onshore Wind
If the wind is too much onshore the waves will strike the board along its full length, washing it back towards the beach and causing the rig to *lose power* as you shoot to leeward, which can drop you into the water. You must combat it by lifting the leeward rail and luffing into the oncoming waves.

Offshore Wind
If the wind is more offshore it is easiest to sail out at an angle. If there are any waves they will strike the leeward rail – you should anticipate them by leaning back to take the *increased* power in the rig as they push you back towards the shore.

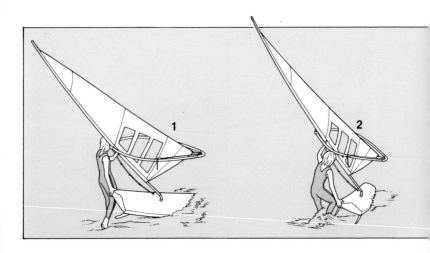

The Beach Start

With a sideshore wind, the neatest way to launch is the beach start.

1. Pick the board up by the tail (a footstrap makes a good hold), and with the other hand hold the rig with one hand on the mast – above or below the wishbone, whichever is easiest. The clew will fly free downwind. Start to slide the board down to the water's edge (on edge may be easiest, but beware of bad scratching if the surface is concrete). Take care not to let the clew dip, or you will be sent flying into the water.

2. Slide the board into the water, until it's deep enough for you to be able to hop on and sail off without hitting the bottom – the daggerboard should be retracted. Drop the tail and place both hands on the wishbone in the normal sailing position. By pushing with the wishbone, the thrust on the mast foot will combat any tendency of the board to luff up into the wind.

3. For an easy start, you want the board angled for a broad reach. Manoeuvre it by pushing (or pulling) with the wishbone until the tail of the board is within easy reach. Step on with your back foot, and pull in with the sheet hand to combat any tendency of the tail sinking or the board luffing.

4. Step up immediately with the front foot, and power off through the waves.

If the wind is more onshore you may have a lot of problems. The beach start will have to be performed very quickly, and it may be best to carry your board out into the surf. This is easiest with a light board. Hold the nearside front strap and support the rig with your head under the wishbone. Drop it, hop on, and sail off.

Coming back to the beach the procedure is reversed. Hop off, grab the tail and mast, and then quickly walk the tail round into the wind in a 180° arc.

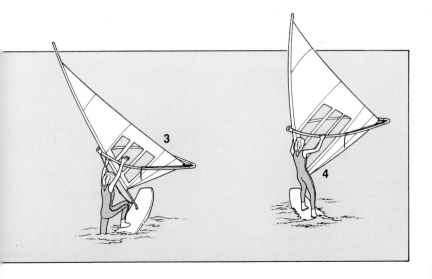

Tacking in Stronger Winds

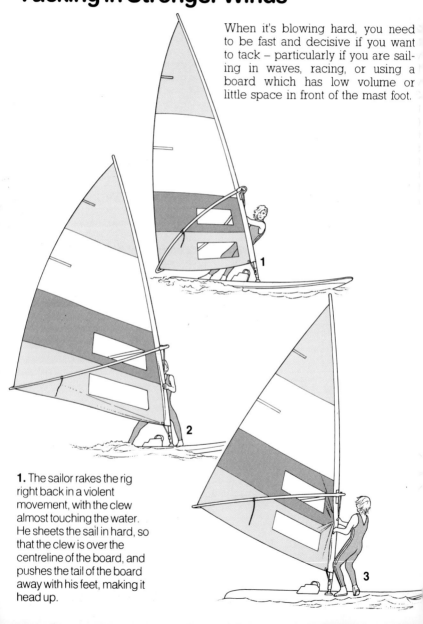

When it's blowing hard, you need to be fast and decisive if you want to tack – particularly if you are sailing in waves, racing, or using a board which has low volume or little space in front of the mast foot.

1. The sailor rakes the rig right back in a violent movement, with the clew almost touching the water. He sheets the sail in hard, so that the clew is over the centreline of the board, and pushes the tail of the board away with his feet, making it head up.

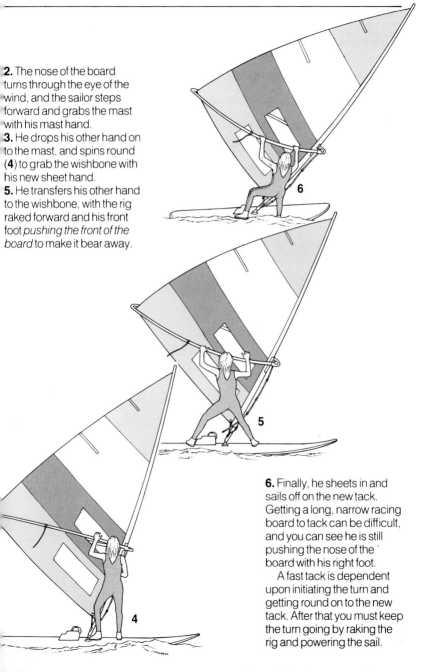

2. The nose of the board turns through the eye of the wind, and the sailor steps forward and grabs the mast with his mast hand.
3. He drops his other hand on to the mast, and spins round (**4**) to grab the wishbone with his new sheet hand.
5. He transfers his other hand to the wishbone, with the rig raked forward and his front foot *pushing the front of the board* to make it bear away.

6. Finally, he sheets in and sails off on the new tack. Getting a long, narrow racing board to tack can be difficult, and you can see he is still pushing the nose of the board with his right foot.

A fast tack is dependent upon initiating the turn and getting round on to the new tack. After that you must keep the turn going by raking the rig and powering the sail.

The Flare Gybe

The best gybe for stronger winds is a *flare gybe*, although it can also be practised in light winds and is frequently used as a freestyle trick.

Its success depends upon banking the rig a long way to windward, sinking the windward rail at the tail, and sailing for a short time clew-first with the wind coming from the leeward side.

With a lot of practice, it is possible to gybe very quickly in a short space using this technique. For this reason it is widely used for tight mark-rounding during races. A good sailor should be able to keep the board under complete control throughout the sequence.

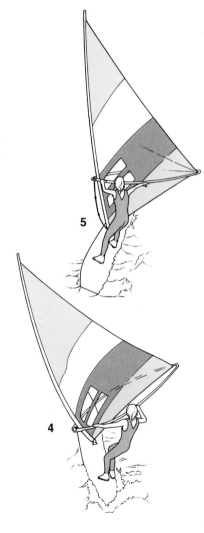

1. Approaching the buoy on a broad reach, the sailor initiates the gybe by banking the rig to windward.

2. The board begins to turn, but he can make the gybe sharper and faster by moving back to stand on the tail of the board and sinking the windward rail.

3. As the tail of the board passes through the eye of the wind, the rig is banked over to at least 45°.

4. He begins sailing *clew-first*, with the wind blowing on to the starboard side of the board. He continues the turn by *powering the rig* and *sinking the tail* (in particular on the windward rail).

5. The turn is completed. The sailor steps forward quickly, releasing his sail hand to let the rig flip round to the new side, but without letting the clew hit the water.

6. His old sheet hand holds the mast, allowing him to grab the boom with his new sheet hand. He moves his hand from the mast to the boom and heads up to sail upwind on the new course.

65

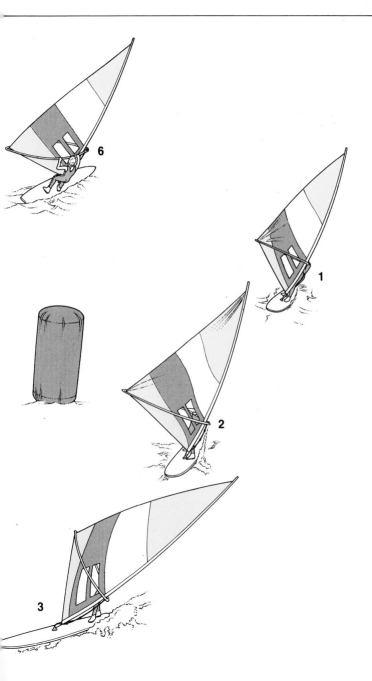

6

1

2

3

Problems and Answers

I have problems getting under way.
Getting under way in strong winds is much easier with a sail that has a high clew and short 6½ft (2m) wishbone. Be decisive. Rake the rig well to windward, grab the wishbone, and sheet in. If the board shows a tendency to luff, push like mad with your front foot to make the nose bear away.

The board luffs when I am sailing.
Rake the rig forward/move the mast/foot forward (a track helps)/ use a HAR sail with a short chord/ sail with bigger skegs and a smaller daggerboard/sheet in.

I am catapulted over the rig.
Let go and fall to windward.

The board rails up.
Use a smaller daggerboard/partially retract the daggerboard/push down the windward rail with your feet.

I am out of control on the run.
Retract the daggerboard – if you can't, pull it/stand on the widest part of the board/squat to keep your weight low/try kneeling or sitting down/let the rig blow in front of you like a flag.

I am out of control on the reach.
Retract the daggerboad/move the skeg to the back of its box.

I am out of control on the beat.
Move the mast foot forward/partially retract the daggerboard/use a smaller sail.

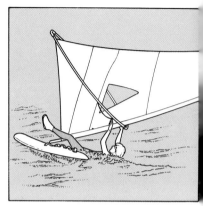

Above: Falling to windward happens when the rig is depowered due to the board luffing up into the wind.

Waterstarts

In waves and strong winds it may be impossible to uphaul a funboard – and it's invariably easier to learn to waterstart.

Swim the rig round so that it's on the windward side of the board (which is facing almost directly into the wind). If the clew is upwind, lift it so the wind catches it and flips it downwind. Raise the rig by pushing up on the mast just above the wishbone – kick with your feet and keep swimming the rig forward.

As soon as the wind gets under it and lifts the clew, get your hands on the boom (sheet hand first). Power the rig and get one foot on to the board. Keep kicking with the other leg; stretch your arms and bend your body to get in over the board; stand up and sail away.

Above: If the rig takes control and catapults you, let go and fall backwards before it's too late. Going with the rig is dangerous, particularly if you're hooked on with a harness – it can lead to a broken mast or head.

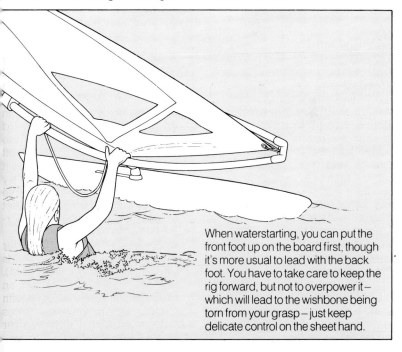

When waterstarting, you can put the front foot up on the board first, though it's more usual to lead with the back foot. You have to take care to keep the rig forward, but not to overpower it – which will lead to the wishbone being torn from your grasp – just keep delicate control on the sheet hand.

Footsteering and the Carve Gybe

The new style of funboards and allround-funboards are recognizable by their footstraps, and by their low volume rounded tails (usually *pintails* with the roundness ending in a point) which allows them to *carve turns* by *footsteering.*

Carving Turns

The technique is quite different from sailing a conventional board. Forget about raking the rig forward and back to make the board turn. If you're going fast enough (you must be planing) and are sailing the right kind of board, you lift the windward rail by pulling up on the front footstrap and pushing down on the leeward rail with the back foot. This sends you into an immediate turn away from the wind, with the board banking like a ski. If you want to turn up *towards the wind,* follow the opposite procedure.

Try the following test to see whether your board is suitable for carving turns by footsteering. Plane on a close reach with your feet tucked into the footstraps. Lift the heel of your front foot and press with the toes of your back foot....

Excellent response throws you and your board into a sweeping curve away from the wind.

Average response means that the board bears away gradually with no rig movement needed apart from sheeting in.

Poor response is when the leeward rail submerges, and there is no change in direction. Only a short board – under 10 ft (3 m) is likely to rate as *excellent.*

The Carve Gybe

The carve gybe is a funboard technique which should be accomplished with only the slightest stall.

1. Start the turn by lifting the windward rail, with the back foot out of the strap and on the leeward rail.

2. Lean into the turn.

3. The tail of the board passes through the eye of the wind. You can perpetuate the turn and prevent the board from stalling, by sailing clew-first.

4. The board has carved through 180° and is ready to reach in the other direction. Let go the wishbone with the sheet hand, grab the mast, and let the rig flip over.

Great skill is needed to prevent a stall before you can sheet in and accelerate off on to a reach again. *This technique is more difficult than it looks.*

Footstraps and Jumps

If you want to make your board jump, footstraps are essential. Take care when using them. They should be soft and comfortable, and should really be called 'toe straps' – only your toes should peek through, for if the straps are too large and your ankle slips through, you could have a nasty accident.

The lighter the board, the easier it will be to get airborne. A board with a fairly wide tail will be easier to jump than one with a slim pintail. You need a good take-off area, and you also need the right conditions.

Jumps are achieved by hitting a suitable ramp so fast that you're bound to take off. After that, the length and height of jumps are decided by the sailor's skill as the wind gets under his board and rig while he's airborne.

If you've got a light board and you're going fast enough, you can jump the tiniest of waves – the wake from a speedboat will be enough to get your board a foot above the surface.

The technique is called *chop jumping.* You start by reaching as fast as possible with your feet in

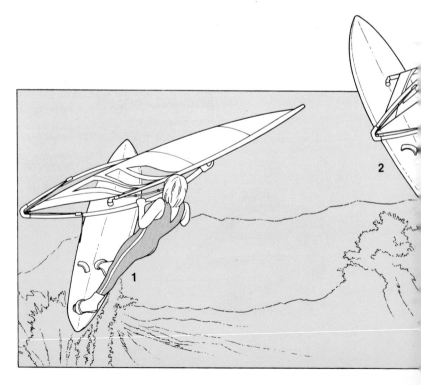

the backstraps to take the weight off the front of the board and to help lift the tail when you take off. Choose your wavelet, and hit it head on – if necessary you must luff viciously at the last moment. At the same time flip the board up on edge, lifting the windward rail so you can get the wind under the board.

As the board takes off, sheet in hard and curl your toes to grip. You can pull the board nearly vertical with an action similar to a quick pull in weightlifting, before letting it down again.

Below: When jumping out through surf from a beach:
1. Aim straight for the oncoming wave and lean towards the tail as the nose lifts. At the last moment before take-off, swing your body in over the board towards the rig.
2. While airborne you can still power the rig, but watch out for leeward drift which can only be reduced by depowering the sail.
3. Aim to land tail first and flex your knees and ankles.

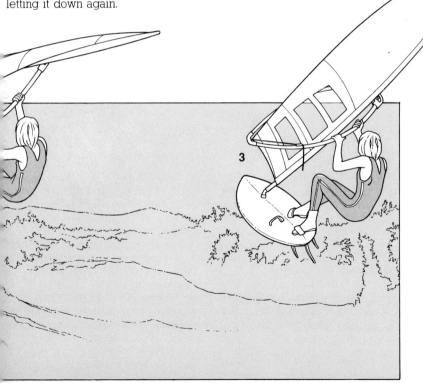

The Duck Gybe

From the basic skills of footsteering and the manoeuvrability of the ultra-short sinker, a remarkable number of highly specialized techniques have evolved.

Most of these were invented by the Hawaiian sailors, who have the advantage of being able to sail in perfect conditions for months on end – big waves, hot sun, and plenty of wind from the Trades.

One of the most popular new techniques is the duck gybe. It was invented by local sailor Richard Whyte when trying to do a *sail 360* (a popular freestyle trick in which

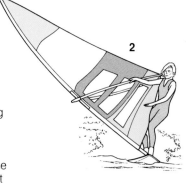

The sequence illustrated here is probably the simplest way of performing a duck gybe:

1. The initial stages are the same as for the carve gybe. Reaching at maximum speed, start to carve a turn away from the wind by lifting on the strap with your front foot. At the same time, press down the leeward rail at the tail with your back foot, which you have already taken out of the strap.

2. The sequence takes place in split seconds. On the approach to a full downwind course, the sailor lets go with his mast hand, letting the rig flip away from him as it describes an arc to windward.

3. He grabs the foot of the sail (some sails are specially made with a handle on the

foot for this purpose) and lets go with his sheet hand so that the mast can pivot as he sweeps his hand, which is holding the foot, from right to left across his body.

4. This manoeuvre has brought the rig into the correct position for sailing on the new tack. By pulling the foot forward, the sailor can reach out and grab the wishbone with his new mast hand, and catch it with his sheet hand. He then completes his turn.

you rotate the rig through 360°) while wavesailing.

The duck gybe is a particularly smooth way of gybing a funboard, with the added advantage that the board can be carved through the turn without stalling. Also, when performed by an expert, the technique looks much slicker and more effortless than the more ordinary carve gybe.

A variety of techniques have been evolved for duck gybing – it is a real case of funboard freestyle. The requirements are a board that has excellent response to carving a turn, and a high clew sail with a short wishbone.

The board is carved through a minimum of 90° up to a maximum of 180° throughout the sequence. The board must keep planing without a stall, so that the apparent wind is a controllable minimum – there should be no power in the sail due to the speed of the board. If it stalls, the apparent wind increases sharply, and the rig may be blown from the sailor's hand.

An even newer technique is the *board 360*, where the sailor carves a turn through 360°.

Safety and Rescue

1. Don't risk an offshore wind if you can't handle it.
2. Check the weather forecast.
3. Learn about the tides.
4. Choose the right size sail.
5. Cold can kill – dress correctly.
6. Windsurfing is unwise for non-swimmers. Either way, wear buoyancy.
7. Check your gear for potential breakages. Carry a towline.
8. Always leash the rig.
9. Let someone know if you're sailing alone.
10. Learn self-help techniques.
11. Know the Rules of the Road.
12. Don't abandon your board, unless getting on a rescue craft.

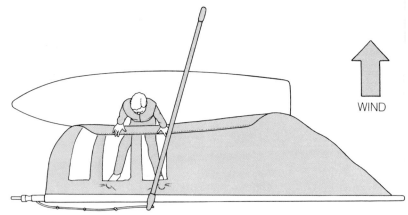

WIND

Above: To roll up the rig, unplug the mast foot and manoeuvre the rig so you're holding the wishbone with the board downwind of it (a board always blows downwind of its rig, which has more drag). Undo the outhaul and roll the sail from the clew (you'll have to remove the battens). When you reach the mast, the sail should be a tight roll. Lash it with the outhaul and uphaul.

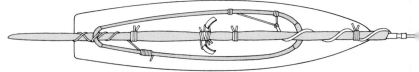

With the wishbone lashed to the rolled sail, place the rig along the centreline of the board with the mast foot facing forward. If you have footstraps you can lash it to the board so that it won't slide around – otherwise you will have real problems, and should dump the rig if necessary.

Self-Help

If you get into difficulty, you can pack up your rig and paddle your board home (above). Either lie on top of the board (as here) or sit astride it.

However, if you have abandoned sailing because you can't handle an offshore wind, you are unlikely to make very much progress. It is painfully slow and if there are waves it's very difficult.

It sometimes makes better sense to stay where you are and give the international distress signal, crossing your hands back and forth across your head (centre).

If rescue is in the form of another board, you can hitch a lift (below). If no help comes, have no compunction about abandoning your rig, but never abandon your board as you try and paddle home.

Rescue is inglorious, timewasting, and it can be expensive. Try and make sure it happens to someone other than yourself. It is usually caused when a sailor is unable to handle the conditions; and occasionally when there is a major breakage such as the rubber coupling in the mast foot.

Taking Up Racing

Windsurfers usually race round a course based on the concept of the *Olympic Triangle* – shown opposite.

It's called an Olympic Triangle because it's used for all the sailboat racing in the Olympic Games, and even if a race organized by local enthusiasts doesn't follow it very exactly, they will always try and include its main elements. These are: starting and finishing the race with beats to windward; equal importance placed on reaching and running; with skill in mark rounding also counting highly.

Almost all windsurfer racing is run to IYRU (International Yacht Racing Union) rules. The main point of these is to avoid collisions (in particular while rounding marks), but they do manage to be extremely complicated. If you want to race seriously it's worth buying a book that is exclusively devoted to the rules of racing (*see* the Bibliography at the back of this book).

Racing Classes
Is your board eligible for this kind of racing? It almost certainly is, and even if it doesn't fit into one of the following categories, you can probably race it at club level on a handicap basis. If there's a large numerical following of one particular brand, it will have its own organized one-design racing.

Most board racing is done on an 'all race as equal' basis. Boards are chosen to race together by measurement or because they are the same brand; they start together, and the first board to finish is the winner. Except at local level, handicap racing is unusual.

The great organizer of the racing classes is the IYRU. There are several 'International' classes which race with their blessing, and between them they probably make up 90% of the racing worldwide.

Open Class
Division I
Division I is for boards that have to be fairly flat, due to a measurement rule that only allows them a maximum 6½ in (16.5 cm) board depth. The intention is that they will appeal to many more people than Division II, but since the IYRU cannot agree on a workable measurement rule, boards in Division I are at present 'homologated' – they're chosen by committee and a list of boards homologated in the UK can be obtained from the RYA, or the USYRA in the USA.

Division II
This is roundboard Open Class with identical measurement rules to Division I, except that the maximum board depth is 8½ in (22 cm), which allows them to be a rounded shape – much faster, but more difficult to sail.

Boards conform to Division II through their measurement rules. The UKBSA (UK Boardsailing Association) is the main organizer of national events in the UK, while IBSA (International Boardsailing Association) organizes the big international regattas such as the World and European Championships.

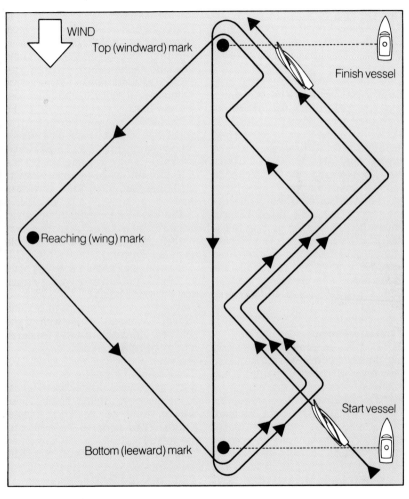

The Olympic Triangle starts with a beat to the windward mark, where the boards bear away for a reach to the wing mark, gybing for another reach to the bottom (leeward) mark. They then beat up to the windward mark again, run back down to the bottom mark, and have a final beat up to the finish which is by the windward mark. The course illustrated is 'port hand' (all marks to port) but it could be run as 'starboard hand'. The race can be shortened by only sailing the first four legs to make a triangle, without the final 'sausage'.

One-Designs

The three International One-Designs are the Windsurfer Regatta, Windglider, and Mistral Competition.

In theory all boards in a one-design class are exactly the same, but in practice all of these marques have been allowed to evolve over the years – they need to keep up with developments and design changes if they are to retain their positions in the highly competitive board market.

The Windsurfer is currently the most popular of the three boards, with a keen following in most major windsurfing countries. The Mistral is the lightest and the quickest (but also the most expensive) while the Windglider was chosen as the first board to be raced in the Olympic Games.

Funboard Racing

As interest in strong wind sailing and funboards has grown, so there has been a move away from the classical Olympic Triangle style of racing. Funboards like reaching, but are not designed for running, and don't like beating. Consequently they need special types of competitions.

Funboard racing is now being organised with limited restrictions (sometimes none at all) on boards and equipment. There is usually a minimum wind requirement of Force 4 (which leads to trouble when there are only light winds at a regatta) and the competition is divided between one or more of the following disciplines:

Course Racing

The course starts with a short beat followed by two long reaches. It finishes with a *slalom* course, reaching and gybing round five closely spaced marks. Duration is 30 minutes at most.

Ins-and-Outs

A knock-out competition sailed by about five boards at a time. They simply reach round and round two marks – ideally one should be inside the surf, while the other is outside the surf – gybing at either end.

The start can be Le Mans style from the beach, or a short reach started on the water if the boards used are *floaters*.

Ins-and-outs should be fast and furious – particularly with waves and breaking surf.

Slalom

Similar to ins-and-outs, with short reaches between closely spaced marks, gybing at every one.

Waves

Wave competitions are *freestyle on the waves*. Two sailors have up to 20 minutes to demonstrate their skill in front of the shore-based judges. They jump, gybe and ride the waves.

These are knock-out competitions with one sailor being eliminated and the other going on to meet the next finalist.

Other Competitions

At major regattas it's normal for organizers to lay on a long distance 'marathon' of 20 miles or more; a knock-out slalom with two competitors sailing at a time; and a freestyle competition.

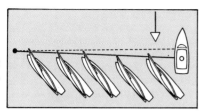

Top: A start line for an Olympic Triangle should face directly into the wind, though it is necessary to have a little bias to give competitors at the port end an even chance. The start sequence is usually a 10 minute gun; five minute gun; one minute gun; and then the off. Each gun is signalled by a flag, and competitors usually time their starts with stop watches. Any board over the line before the start gun has to go back and start again, while keeping clear of everyone else.

Below: The funboard racing course is a squashed and elongated version of the Olympic Triangle. The beat is very short; the reaches are very long; and the run is transformed into a reaching and gybing slalom.

Below: The boards on a funboard slalom sail a figure-of-eight course round two marks, so that they reach in and out through the surf. They can start on the water, but in top racing it's usual to do this kind of racing on sinkers which are fastest on a reach and have the most manoeuvrability. Therefore they usually start Le Mans style from the water's edge, and complete the course by running up to a finish line on the beach. There are a maximum of eight competitors sailing about five laps round the marks, which they can do in a matter of minutes.

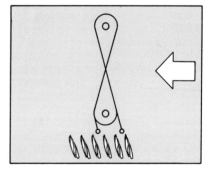

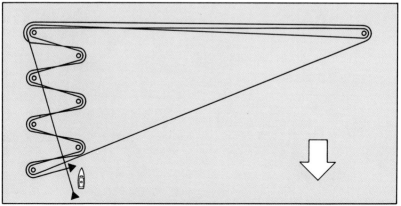

Freestyle

Freestyle is doing tricks on a board. You can either do them for fun (showing off) or as part of a three-minute competition routine. The judges mark on the number of tricks, their difficulty, the originality of the routine, and your style throughout.

The ideal board for freestyle is flat with wide, deep rails. It should be stable and easy to sail, but at the same time responsive and quick to manoeuvre. Typical favourites are the Windsurfer Regatta and Mistral Competition – they frequently have cut-down skegs to help them turn quickly.

Ideal conditions for learning freestyle are flat water with Force 2-3. The mast foot must be fixed securely, and the board must have good non-slip, You'll find it easiest with a medium size high clew sail.

The tricks and variations are endless. There are pirouettes, duck tacks, head dips, sail 360s and tail sinks – but the ultimate has to be the railride.

The Basic Railride

This is the trick everyone would like to do. Before you start, it is vital that the mast foot is tightly wedged. Force 3 is the best wind to give you enough power in the sail. You can practise on dry land, learning to balance the board on edge on the beach – when you can do that, it's time to take to the water.

1. Sail across the wind, and lift the windward rail with your front foot, pressing down the leeward rail with the other.

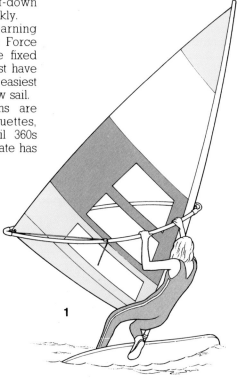

1

2. Get the feel of tilting the board, until you are ready to tilt it all the way on to the rail. Move your hands back along the wishbone to keep the rig forward and prevent luffing. Lift your front foot and press with your back foot until the board comes up against the mast. As it does so, lean your shin on the top rail while you slide your back foot up there with it. Balance the board by sheeting in to prevent it falling to windward. Push with your shin to prevent it falling to leeward.

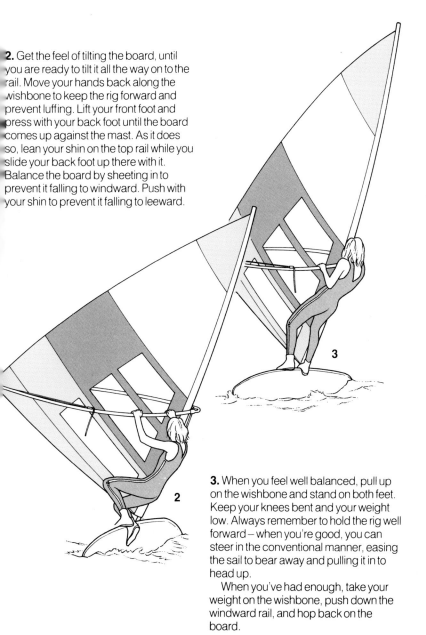

3. When you feel well balanced, pull up on the wishbone and stand on both feet. Keep your knees bent and your weight low. Always remember to hold the rig well forward – when you're good, you can steer in the conventional manner, easing the sail to bear away and pulling it in to head up.

When you've had enough, take your weight on the wishbone, push down the windward rail, and hop back on the board.

Care of Boards and Sails

Sails

Sails probably get least wear when they're actually sailing. It's when they're ashore that they are most at risk. Points to note are:

1. Dragging the sail over the beach or concrete is a bad idea. It will remove the protective finish from the cloth and wear out the top of the mast tube.

2. When you're launching or coming ashore in breaking waves, try and keep the rig clear of the water. Sudden heavy loads can do a great deal of damage.

3. When de-rigging, let the downhaul off first. You must never overload the luff.

4. Salt on a sail attracts moisture, and keeps it damp when you store it, which will cause the finish on the cloth to break down. Always hose off any salt with fresh water if you've been sailing on the sea.

5. Try and dry the sail before storing it away. The best way is to stand the rig up with the sail under tension. Never leave it flapping in the wind – it will break down the finish.

Storing Sails

It's not harmful to leave the sail rolled on the mast, so long as it is dry and the downhaul is released.

If you need to take the sail off the mast, always *flake* it, using the technique shown in the illustration below. If the sail is Mylar, it is preferable to roll it, since great care must be taken not to crack the finish. The easiest way is to roll the sail round a plastic pipe with the tack and clew tied at either end.

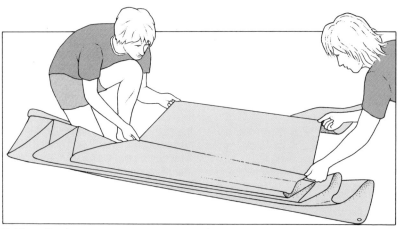

Fold a sail by flaking it along the seams or parallel with them. It's easiest if two people do it, with one on the luff and one on the leech. Avoid putting creases in the windows, and finish by rolling the flaked sail from the leech to the luff. It will then fit in a bag. Particular care should be taken with a Mylar sail.

When it's rolled tight, it will then fit inside a larger pipe for storage at home or on your roof rack.

Cleaning

Tar stains are a problem on any beach. You must act immediately, getting as much as possible off with a knife; then use petrol or one of the proprietary brands of sail cleaner available from chandleries.

Wash off everything that's left with soap and water, and then rinse thoroughly. Unfortunately it's difficult to remove every trace of tar stain.

Ordinary soap and water is best for general cleaning. Never scrub the sail; keep clear of washing machines; and beware of the effect of washing powders which may damage the finish. If in doubt, leave it dirty.

If you want to change racing numbers, you can remove the old glue with *Acetone* – a special solvent, available from chemists. This does not harm the sail, but will ruin a carpet – so take care when you use it!

Care and Repair

A small tear which is not attended to can quickly turn into a major job for your sailmaker. Suitable sticky tape can be adequate for a permanent repair.

The mast tube is vulnerable, and the most difficult part of the sail to repair.

Skegs rip holes in sails on the beach – never leave the clew of your rig upwind, or it may blow over on to a skeg.

Board Repairs

Polyethylene is considered the most durable of windsurfer skin materials, but has the disadvantage that it's virtually impossible to repair yourself – unless you have and know how to use a hot air welding gun.

In the unlikely event of knocking a hole in your polyethylene board, you must stop water entering the foam by covering it with tough, waterproof tape – then take it to a specialist.

ABS boards have a habit of splitting round the seam where the two halves of the hull join. A reasonably permanent repair can be made with a tube of liquid ABS (available from windsurfing shops) which is also suitable for Polycoren (Mistral), but not for ASA – use tape followed by the services of a specialist.

Glassfibre boards made with Polyester resin have a high gloss gel coat which is easy to chip. Fortunately it is easy to repair with a filler such as *Plastic Padding* – though you must always clean and dry the damage first.

Glassfibre boards made with epoxy resin can have small holes filled with *Araldite Rapid* – anything more extensive requires specialist treatment.

Whatever the skin material, always protect the foam core. If it gets wet, it may be impossible to dry out. It is of course possible to do specialist repairs yourself, but consult the supplier/manufacturer just in case you're about to make an expensive mistake.

Windsurfing Holidays

There are holiday packages available in most of the desirable corners of the world – generally that means the places where it's warm and where there's wind. Some of them are shown on the map.

You should check whether the holiday just happens to include windsurfing, or has been specifically designed around it. If you're an advanced sailor, the boards and equipment may be unsuitable for your requirements, which means

that you will have to travel with your own gear.

Two uninterrupted weeks of warm conditions are the perfect way to learn windsurfing. You should make sure that any school

you attend issues a proper IWS Certificate (*see* page 86) or the equivalent – in a few countries you may actually need a certificate before you're allowed to hire a board. If you're into racing, big interna-

tional regattas are a great way to travel. Most of the major classes run their European and World Championships in exotic places, and tend to provide a subsidized package, with all the equipment already there.

Schools and Tuition

The best way to learn windsurfing is to take an approved course. There are schools offering these courses all over the world, most of which are based on the original IWS (International Windsurfer Schools) format.

The IWS system was evolved by Dagobart Benz. He taught himself to windsurf when the first board appeared, but realized that guests at his hotel on Lake Constance (West Germany) would need a proper step-by-step system of teaching.

Before long he had set up IWS schools all over Europe, having started a pyramid of instructors teaching pupils who in turn became instructors – and still continue to do so.

Many national authorities run teaching systems based on the IWS (in the UK it's the RYA) which award *certificates of competence*.

The IWS Course

The typical IWS syllabus will follow these lines:

1. Duration

About eight hours. It can be compressed into a single day or strung out over a weekend or longer. If the weather is unsuitable, you would expect to come back another time.

2. Facilities

The price should include the cost of the course with properly qualified instruction, use of a board and a suitable wetsuit and buoyancy aid, as well as a powered rescue craft on hand at all times. Some schools can obviously offer considerably grander facilities than others, which may be reflected in the price.

3. Format

A course revolves around *theory* and *practice*. This will include: tuition in a classroom; on a dry land simulator; and on the water.

By the end of the course you should be able to rig the board and sail it around a small triangular course (ie in any direction) in light winds with a small sail, and have basic knowledge of seamanship and safety.

4. Certificate

If you pass the above requirements (most do) you are issued with a Certificate of Competence.

Advanced Courses

As windsurfing techniques grow more sophisticated, there is growing demand for advanced tuition. As yet there are no formal teaching systems, but it is possible to find this type of tuition in the UK (contact the RYA, UKBSA, or a local windsurf shop) as well as further afield. You would expect to learn anything ranging from racing tactics to funboard techniques such as the waterstart and duck gybe, with tuition from a real expert.

Fireside Tuition

There are specialist books on the racing rules and racing, freestyle, building your own board, funboard techniques, and the weather.

Nowadays, there are also an increasing number of videos, ranging from basic learn-to-windsurf to shots of the stars in action.

The windsurfing simulator is a marvellous device which has evolved through the IWS system. It enables you to practise the basics of windsurfing without going near the water and getting wet every time you fall off.

The simulator can range from the basic to the sophisticated, as long as it represents the middle section of the deck of a windsurfer, mounted on an articulated turntable, and with a rig plugged into it.

As such it's every bit as difficult as standing on a board in choppy water, and you can practise uphauling the rig, turning the board, and simulated sailing – all the time under the critical eye of your instructor.

Windsurfing Magazines

UK
Boards
Yachting Press Ltd
196 Eastern Esplanade
Southend on Sea
Essex

On Board
28 Parkside
Wollaton
Nottingham

Windsurf
Ocean Publications Ltd
34 Buckingham Palace Road
London SW1

France
Planche
5 rue du Commandant Pilot
92522 Neuilly Cedex

Planche à Voile
5 rue du Commandant Pilot
92522 Neuilly Cedex

Wind
52 Boulevard Sebastopol
75003 Paris

Germany
Funboard
Sachsenkamstrasse 19
Postfach 801008
8000 München 70

Surf
Sachsenkamstrasse 19
Postfach 801008
8000 München 70

Surfen
Prinzregentstrasse 124
8000 München 80

Netherlands
Surf
Postbus 125
1000 AC Amsterdam

Italy
Surf
Via Tradino 29
20124 Milano

Windsurf
Viale Regina Margherita 2
20122 Milano

Norway
Brett Seilas
Postboks 5928
Hegdehaugen
Oslo 3

USA
Sailboarder
33046 Calle Aviador
San Juan Capistrano
CA 92675

Windrider
1211 Palmetto Avenue
Winter Park
FL 32789

Wind Surf
24581 Del Prado
Dana Point
CA 92629

Canada
Windsport
PO Box 308
Clarkson
Mississauga
Ontario

Japan
Windflash
Takenaka Three Bldg. 102
2-18-2, Minami-Aoyama
Minato-ku
Tokyo

Useful Addresses

1. International Bodies

IYRU
60 Knightsbridge
London SW1
Tel: 01-235 6221
The International Yacht Racing Union is the backbone of yacht racing throughout the world. With a few exceptions, such as professional and funboard racing, most windsurfing regattas are run to IYRU rules.

IBSA
PO Box 1710
CH-3001 Bern
Switzerland
The International Boardsailing Association founded the Open Class and did all the initial development work on Division II. They have run all the World and European Championships for this class since its inception in 1979.

WSMA
Feldafinger Platz 2
D 8000 München 71
West Germany
The World Sailboard Manufacturers Association was formed to run the first World Funboard Cup series in 1983, which is the closest windsurfing has come to a professional Grand Prix circuit. Venues for the WSMA regattas include Australia, Hawaii, USA (San Francisco); and in Europe, France (north-west Brittany), Germany (the island of Sylt), and the Netherlands (Scheveningen on the North Sea). Members include Mistral, Fanatic, Sailboard, Bic, Tiga, Hi Fly, F2; and the sailmakers North, Gaastra, and Hy Line.

2. International Class Associations

IWCA
The Secretary
1955 West 190th St
Torrance CA 90509
USA
The International Windsurfer Class Association has the greatest number of members who race one-design, with World, European, and National Championships that are always extremely popular.

IWGCA
Rottink Travel Agency Building
Prinses Irenestraat 31
1077 WV Amsterdam
Netherlands
The International Windglider Class Association is the only one to boast membership behind the Iron Curtain. The Windglider was the IYRUs choice for the 1984 Olympic Games.

IMCO
Herengracht 52P
1015 BN
Amsterdam
Netherlands
The International Mistral Class Organization organizes racing for the one-design Mistral Competition, which is available in various weights down to 33lb (15kg) Superlight.

3. UK National Bodies

RYA
Victoria Way
Woking, Surrey
Tel: 048 62 5022
The Royal Yachting Association acts as the governing body of yachting in the UK. It has a Boardsailing Committee, and is heavily involved in competitions which include the Weymouth Speed Trials; and in teaching, with a course that has evolved from the IWS system.

UKBSA
Masons Road
Stratford-upon-Avon
Warwickshire
Tel: 0789 299574

The United Kingdom Boardsailing Association is the biggest windsurfing association in the UK. It is primarily involved in running Open Class regattas.

Scottish Boardsailing Association
c/o Graphic Partners
179 Cannongate
Edinburgh
Tel: 031 557 3558

Run on similar lines to the UKBSA

Records

The windsurfing world speed record is run over a 500 metre (547 yard) course. The most important speed trials are all held in Europe in the autumn – in Brest (north-west France), Portland Harbour (near Weymouth in the South of England), and Veere (Netherlands) – with the RYA acting as observers at each event.

1977
17.1 knots
Derk Thijs of the Netherlands on a Windglider – it had foam removed to make it lighter, and the daggerboard case was sealed.

1979
19.2 knots
Clive Colenso won the record for Britain, sailing a standard Olympic Gold.

1980
24.45 knots

Jaap van der Rest of the Netherlands demolished the record at special speed trials held on Maalaea Bay, on the Hawaiian island of Maui. He sailed a special board designed by Gary Seaman.

1981
25.2 knots
The first use of surfboard sinkers pushed up the record. Jaap used one to set a new record at Veere.

1982
27.82 knots
Frenchman Pascal Maka bumped the record up at Portland.

1983
30.82 knots
Fred Haywood came with a special team from Hawaii and annihilated the record. He used a carbon fibre 'wing' mast which superseded conventional rigs.

Racing

The Open Class
Divisions 1 and 2
Divisions 1 and 2 (flatboard and roundboard) have virtually the same measurement specifications, with the major exception of the depth of board: Division 1 is not more than 16.5 cm; Division 2 is not more than 22 cm.

The full Division 1 and 2 rules can be obtained from the IYRU. They can be summarized as follows:
Overall length: 3920 cm max.
Beam at widest point: 630 mm min.
Other beam restrictions: Not less than 590 mm for lengths of 1300 mm.
Depth of board: Not more than 165 mm.

Division 1: Not more than 220 cm.

Division 2: Weight of board: 18 kg min.

Daggerboard: 700 cm max depth from underside of board.

Skeg: 300 mm max.

Mast: 4700 mm max.

Buoyancy: The Division 2 board shall either have three watertight compartments dividing its total volume into approximately equal parts, or a minimum of 0.1 cubic metres of rigid closed cell foam. The Division 1 board shall be entirely filled with rigid closed cell plastic foam of approved density.

Safety: A towing eye and mast leash must be fitted. There shall be no sharp upward projecting edges of radius less than 15 mm.

Materials: High modulus fibres such as Kevlar are prohibited.

Footstraps: Prohibited.

Limitation of equipment: During a race meeting only one board, two sails, and two daggerboards may be used. The board shall not be altered in any way during the race meeting.

Harness: Permitted.

Compass: Permitted.

Weight Groups: Two are recommended. IBSA break at 71 kg, while the UKBSA break at 72 kg.

Division 1 and 2 Sails

Division 1 and 2 sails have the same specifications and are interchangeable:

Luff	4400 mm
Leech	4300
Head to mid foot	4300
¾ height width	940
½ height width	1680
¼ height width	2270
Foot	2580

Division 1 Homologation

Division 2 is open to any one-off prototype, or production board that satisfies the measurement rules.

Division 1 is restricted to:

A. An IYRU International Class ie Windsurfer, Windglider, Mistral.

B. A class approved by the IYRU of which there are not less than 2000 similar boards satisfying the measurement rules. NB. when Division 1 was introduced into the UK in 1982, no classes (apart from the three International Classes) satisfied B. Therefore the RYA hold trials and 'homologate' Division 1 boards. In the USA the USYRU do likewise.

Division 3

Open Class Division 3 covers tandems. The measurement specifications and class rules are similar to Division 2, with the very obvious exception that Division 3 allows two rigs and two drivers! There are also the following main differences:

Overall length: 6800 mm max.

Beam at widest point: Not less than 650 mm/not more than 750 mm.

Depth of board: Not more than 250 mm.

Weight of board: 50 kg min.

Daggerboard: 910 cm max depth from underside of board.

Scoring

Most regattas use the IYRU's Olympic scoring system which gives the following points to each finisher:

1st	0 points
2nd	3 points
3rd	5.7 points
4th	8 points
5th	10 points
6th	11.7 points
7th etc	Place plus 6 points.

The lowest total score wins. When there are seven races the best six shall count; when there are six the best five shall count; when there are five the best four shall count – and a minimum number of five is needed to constitute a series.

In the event of a tie, the tie is broken in favour of the board with the most first places, or most second places, and so on.

Sail Sizes

When buying a sail, the following guide gives some indication as to the right size:

Area	Ladies	Lightweights	Heavyweights
4.0 sq m	Force 4-6	Force 5-7	Force 5-8
4.5 sq m	Force 3-5	Force 4-6	Force 4-7
5.0 sq m	Force 2-4+	Force 3-5+	Force 4-6+
5.5 sq m	Force 0-4	Force 2-5	Force 3-6
6.0 sq m	Force 0-3	Force 0-4	Force 2-5
7.0 sq m	Force 0-2	Force 0-3	Force 0-4
8.0 sq m	Not recommended	Force 0-2+	Force 0-3+

Bibliography

The Complete Guide to Windsurfing
Jeremy Evans (Bell & Hyman)
'The definitive manual for British windsurfers.' (The Times).
Magnificent colour photographs by Alastair Black plus clear and straightforward 'how-to-do-it' drawings. The first half of the book is aimed mainly at beginners: the second half is designed for the more advanced sailor and includes specialist sections by international experts.

The Rules Book
Eric Twiname (Granada)
Paul Elvstrom Explains the Yacht Racing Rules
Paul Elvstrom (Creagh-Osborne & Partners)
Two small books that explain the IYRU racing rules clearly and concisely. Worthwhile for anyone who wants to race seriously.

Windsurfing Racing Technique
Philip Pudenz and Karl Messmer (Stanford Maritime)
A guide to racing, primarily around the Olympic Triangle.

Board Racing
Geoff Turner and Tim Davidson (Fernhurst)
Concerned primarily with Open Class racing on a national level.

Dee Caldwell's Book on Freestyle Boardsailing
Dee Caldwell (Fernhurst)
A simple primer on freestyle – probably the best of the books available on the subject.

Sailboards Custom Made
Hansi Fichtner (Stanford Maritime)
How to make a custom board (now a little out of date).

La Planche A Voile Avec Jenna De Rosnay
Arnaud de Rosnay and Hervé Hauss (Gallimard)
A spectacular coffee table book on how to become the fastest woman in the world.

Weather Lore for Sailors and Windsurfers
Gunther Roth (EP)
A useful primer on weather.

Index